About the Author

Alicia Eaton is a qualified Clinical Hypnotherapist and Licensed Master Practitioner of Neuro-Linguistic Programming® and an Advanced Therapeutic Specialist™ with The Society of NLP. She has run a successful practice in London's Harley Street since 2004. Personally trained to the highest level by Richard Bandler (co-creator of NLP), Paul McKenna and Michael Neill, she has also worked as an assistant to Paul McKenna on his seminars for many years. She has three grown-up children and lives in Hertfordshire.

'When you have a problem you just want it "fixed", you do not need to spend weeks or months understanding or analysing the problem . . . all you need is a fix. There are a few therapists and practitioners around who can deliver this fix and Alicia is indeed one of them. Fixing issues and finding solutions is her trademark'
Kevin Laye, therapist, international trainer, speaker and author of *Positive Shrinking and Positive Drinking*

'Alicia is a colleague of mine and I have had the pleasure of knowing and working with her for several years. Her knowledge and experience enables her to get the best out of her clients, getting results that move them forwards to their highest potential'
Michele Paradise – 'the Bridal Coach' & NLP Trainer

'If you are stranded on a desert island a book on brain surgery will not be very helpful, but a First Aid book might just save your life. We all have our own unique personalities and emotional baggage that slows us down. Hopefully we also have a belief that there is a better future out there waiting for us, but we don't know where to look or how to find it. '*Fix Your Life*' might not save your life but it will certainly help you find the life you deserve. It is easy to read, entertaining, practical and meticulously researched. It will be my desert island book - First Aid for whatever the day brings'
Dr Stephen Simpson – 'the Golf Doctor' and NLP trainer

FIX YOUR LIFE

. . . with NLP

Alicia Eaton

SIMON &
SCHUSTER

London · New York · Sydney · Toronto · New Delhi

A CBS COMPANY

First published in Great Britain in 2012 by Simon & Schuster UK Ltd
A CBS COMPANY

1 3 5 7 9 10 8 6 4 2

Simon & Schuster UK Ltd
1st Floor
222 Gray's Inn Road
London
WC1X 8HB

www.simonandschuster.co.uk

Simon & Schuster Australia, Sydney

Simon & Schuster India, New Delhi

A CIP catalogue copy for this book is available
from the British Library.

ISBN: 978-0-85720-377-9

Illustrations © Liane Payne
Typeset by Hewer Text UK Ltd, Edinburgh
Printed and bound in Great Britain by CPI Group (UK) Ltd,
Croydon, CRO 4YY

The information contained in this book is intended to be educational
and not for diagnosis, prescription or treatment of any kind of health
disorder whatsoever. This information should not replace consultation
with a competent health care professional. The content of this book is
intended to be used as an adjunct to a rational and responsible health
care programme prescribed by a health care practitioner. The author
and publisher are in no way liable for any misuse of the material.

For my children:
George, Tom and Clementine

Acknowledgements

Thank you to Dr Richard Bandler, co-creator of NLP – the ideas and techniques used in this book are based on his developments and I am very fortunate to have been trained by him.

A very special thank you to Paul McKenna for giving me the opportunity to work with him on his seminars and learn so much over the past few years.

I'd also like to thank Michael Neill, Mark Hayley, Gabe Guerrero and Eric Robbie – for putting the polish on my skills.

Thank you to Andrew Lownie, my agent, and to Kerri Sharp and Jane Pizzey at Simon & Schuster.

And to my clients – thank you for sharing your stories with me.

Contents

Introduction

Over the years I've helped hundreds of people change their lives for the better, using the techniques of Neuro-Linguistic Programming, or NLP as it's more commonly known. I've been very fortunate to have been able to learn from and work alongside one of the original creators of NLP – Richard Bandler and also Paul McKenna.

As well as seeing clients in my consulting room in Harley Street, I've spent many years assisting Paul with the seminars put on by his training company. The success and popularity of his books has created a whole new generation of people eager to learn about the magical methodology known as NLP. It's currently the fastest growing type of psychological therapy, and the reason it's so popular is down to the successful results it easily produces.

The majority of books about NLP, however, are heavily academically referenced, making it difficult for ordinary people to take advantage of the many benefits. *Fix Your Life*, on the other hand, cuts through the technical jargon and will enable you to easily understand how you can solve many of your day-to-day problems, putting yourself onto a fast track to success.

Whether you're seeking to give your life a complete make-over or are simply looking for a solution to an irritating habit, you can completely change your life by learning and understanding what makes your mind tick.

Here's what some of my clients have been saying:

'I have a successful job, plenty of money and a loving family. I don't want to change my life – I just want to sort out my fear of heights so I can enjoy my skiing holidays more. And I'm going away next week so can I do it quickly please?'

'I've heard about NLP and how effective it can be to make changes, but I haven't got the time to sit down and learn about it in detail . . . can you just show me what I need to do to feel less anxious in my business meetings?'

'NL what? I'm not sure about that, I'm just really keen to lose weight – I know what to do: eat less and move more, it's not rocket science. But I just can't seem to get myself off the sofa . . . how can I motivate myself? What do I need to do?'

'A friend told me to try NLP to sort out my fear of flying, but I feel like I need a degree in Psychology just to understand it all. How can it help me?'

No-one needs to sit and study in order to learn how to use the same techniques and strategies that are employed by some of the most successful people in the world. When clients come to see me with their problems, I have to work fast – a session lasts around an hour and a half. There's no time for long, fancy explanations – they just want to know how to 'do it'. And in this book, I'm going to show you how you can 'do it' too.

This book will teach you how to become the architect of your future – for the first time, you'll be able to design the kind of life you'd like to have, rather than putting up with the life you just happened to get.

Unlike conventional psychotherapies, which require time and money, you can learn how to do the NLP techniques for yourself. It's my aim to put *you* back in control of your life.

1

Fix Your Life

It's often said that our minds are like computers, but in fact the opposite is true – computers are like our minds. Computer scientists look closely at how the human brain works and design their information processing systems to operate in similar ways. Even the digital imaging software built into your camera was based on the workings of the human eye.

And just like computers, it's not uncommon for us to sometimes pick up a virus. By that I mean accidentally 'download' an unwanted pattern of behaviour. Whether your problem is a fear of flying, a phobia of public speaking or a bad habit like smoking or eating too much – make no mistake, you were not born with your problems. You accidentally downloaded them into your operating software somewhere along the way and you've simply been putting up with them because you didn't realise you could *fix* them!

When computers stop working efficiently, we don't hesitate to call in the experts to clean things up and get them running smoothly once more.

In fact, most of us take better care of our computers than we do of our minds, for we'll quite happily install anti-virus software to prevent problems from occurring and even pay for annual service contracts. We expect them to develop problems over time and sooner or later require fixing.

If we took the same approach to our minds, we'd find them working more efficiently for us and we'd have fewer problems in our lives. 'Servicing' our minds from time to time and erasing unwanted patterns of behaviour should be a habit we adopt for our future health.

Think back to the last time you fell ill, perhaps with a cold or flu or even with an upset stomach. And what about a minor injury: putting your back out, say, or spraining your ankle. Like most people, you probably took action to put yourself back onto the road to recovery. Painkillers, a hot bath, ice packs, support bandages, an early night, rest and relaxation, honey and lemon, homeopathy – the options are endless.

When it comes to our minds, though, we tend to shy away from doing anything to help ourselves. We get trapped in a pattern of bad habits, struggling to lose weight or quit smoking. We allow our lives to be ruled by feelings of fear as we pick up phobias and live a life of anxiety, pretending they're not there. We fail exams, avoid travel and find it difficult to pluck up the courage to get a new job.

Whilst we've become pretty adept at self-diagnosing our physical ailments via the internet, we still have a tendency to feel that 'matters of the mind' should only be dealt with by professionals. But even then there's the worry about whether we can find someone we trust, never mind the commitment of time and money, so we opt to leave things alone. This fear of dabbling leaves us limping through life with minds drastically in need of a 'service'. We accept our limitations and believe there's nothing we can do to improve the situation.

And again, so many of us treat our computers far better. We'll happily download apps – those additional software applications that extend the functions of our equipment beyond the original manufacturer's intention.

How good would it be if we had a set of 'apps for the mind'?

Take a few moments to imagine just that. If you could download an app for your mind right now, what would you choose? An app that wouldn't necessarily change you, but would simply enable you to become a more sophisticated version of who you are right now. What additional capabilities would you choose? Who would you be and where would you go?

Sounds too good to be true? Well, through this book you're going to be able to do just that, for I'm going to show you how you can start to take control of your own mind rather than leaving other people or events to control it for you.

NLP in Practice

Over the years, I've seen literally hundreds of clients in my NLP and hypnotherapy practice in London's Harley Street.

Remember This

Just as you'd download an app for your phone or computer, it really is now possible to download an 'app' for your mind.

NLP is the fastest-growing psychological methodology for very good reasons – it can produce results quicker than most other types of psychological interventions. I've been fortunate to have been trained by three of the world's experts in the field of 'success and changework': Richard Bandler (co-creator of NLP), Paul McKenna and Michael Neill. I've studied their methods in detail and used the same techniques with my clients.

With its worldwide reputation for clinical excellence, Harley Street attracts many people. Some of them are wealthy and seeking the best money can buy, but others come in desperation – it's their last resort. Having searched for a solution to their problems for many years and tried everything else on offer, they are prepared to give the strange-sounding therapy a go. Some of them are prepared to travel miles across the country and even come from abroad, such is the shortage of good, highly qualified NLP practitioners. I've seen how difficult it's been for many of my clients to get access to good-quality help and information about the subject and I've written this book to change that situation.

My clients have ranged in age from three to 83 years old, such is the flexible nature of the strategies and techniques. Whether your problem is an irritating little habit such as nail-biting, a fear of public speaking, an inability to shift that extra weight or a full-blown emotional trauma, there's something in NLP that will help you to take back control over your life.

Because NLP doesn't simply fix problems, but can also be used as a communication model that enhances relationships – be they personal or business – it's been widely used in the corporate world for many years. Looking for that extra special something that will give their employees the edge over their competitors, many companies are prepared to pay the fees required to buy in expensive training courses. As a result, NLP has almost become a business that's excluded those who are unable to pay for it – the main reason why it's been slow to filter through for use with ordinary everyday situations. So many more of us could benefit from learning how to use it, not to mention all the teachers, doctors, dentists and other health professionals who could apply it to their work in all sorts of situations.

The aim of this book is to make NLP much more accessible to ordinary people. It can be as complicated or as simple you choose to make it and I've cut out the technical jargon that you'll find in most other NLP books. It's not necessary to have a degree or spend many months studying it in order to make it work for you.

NLP will teach you about the mechanics of your mind and enable you to fix those irritating little 'mind problems' that we all unavoidably pick up through life. Just as your car collects miscellaneous scratches, dents and scrapes over the years, so does your mind – it's only natural, and dealing with them is now easier than it ever has been.

We are the lucky ones, for thanks to the sophisticated advances in scanning equipment and the scientific research of neuro-psychologists, we are able to understand more about how our minds work than ever before. And you belong to a generation that can make good use of that knowledge and get your mind working in the way you'd like it to.

Never before has it been more possible to completely take charge of your life and steer it in the direction you'd like it to go. Never before has it been so easy to fix problems and make your life the kind of life you want.

With the prescription of anti-depressants rapidly increasing, it's clear that our bodies are becoming more stressed and our minds more depressed than ever before. We need to find new ways to deal with the pressures of modern life. Consider this book to be your 'first-aid kit' for the mind. For the first time, you'll be able to deal with problems as soon as they occur.

Life in the Twenty-first Century

There's no doubt that our lives are speeding up, requiring us to think and respond quicker than we ever have before. We can now communicate with each other and send instant messages around the world in a flash. Each new year brings with it a fresh crop of technological gadgets: mobile phones, messengers, emails, MP3 players, iPods and iPads. Think how you were communicating with people just ten years ago and compare it to the way you do it now.

How much faster does your mind have to work to absorb all this new information and how much more work are you required to get through each day, as this technology makes your life 'easier'?

Your mind is absorbing information and making decisions far quicker than any of your ancestors did. And throughout this process, your brain has not simply acquired additional knowledge; it has also changed shape. Our brains mould themselves in response to the experiences they encounter and your thoughts leave imprints on your mind.

Scientists call this 'neural plasticity', and just like a piece of plastic that can be fashioned into almost anything, it's possible to actually change the microscopic structure of your brain. Unlike your body, which stops growing after twenty years or so, your brain doesn't. It still has the capacity to grow new neural connections and, like a muscle, it can grow thicker the more we use it.

But as our brains adapt and mould themselves more quickly than ever, in response to the speeding pace of new developments in our society, it's not surprising that from time to time we develop problems with our 'operating software' – a virus, so to speak.

We know that bad experiences that last only a few minutes, such as a traumatic visit to the dentist, being frightened by a large dog or trapped in a lift, can produce a fear or phobia that will last for many years, if not an entire lifetime. Experiences such as these can become deeply imprinted onto our minds as quick as a flash, so it makes sense to 'unimprint' those experiences just as quickly, rather than leaving them there or undergoing months, if not years, of therapy.

There are critics of NLP who believe that all psychological problems should be dealt with in more conventional ways with the use of longer-term psychotherapies, but I believe the quicker interventions of NLP are not only desirable but also more suited to the new type of minds we have. Using specific NLP exercises can reshape your mind, keeping it fitter and healthier for life in the twenty-first century.

So many of our day-to-day problems are small enough not to warrant a visit to a therapist and yet still big enough to make life difficult for us. Things like being overweight, a fear of flying, exam stress or a lack of confidence all contribute to holding us back from living the kind of lives we'd love to have.

Just imagine having the capabilities to change and fashion your mind in the way you want. Who would *you* be if you weren't who you are right now? What kind of things would you be able to do? How would you look? Who would be your friends? What kind of job would you have?

Never before has making those changes been easier.

How to Use this Book: Your First-aid Kit for the Mind

The early chapters of this book will give you an insight into how your mind works: how information is absorbed and processed into thoughts and behaviour. You'll also be able to learn exactly what NLP is and its history. Following the exercises and activities in this section will enable you to prep your mind for solving your problems with the NLP techniques.

Chapters 9 to 13 look at five problem areas in more detail: habit and motivation; weight loss; confidence; fears and phobias; health and wellbeing. As well as picking up tips and ideas, you'll be able to read some of my clients' stories and see how easy it can be to make changes using the techniques.

In Chapter 14 you will find your 'Apps for the Mind'. I've taken well-known NLP techniques and packaged them up in a way that's going to be easy for you to use and, quite literally, download into your mind.

'Downloading the apps' in this book will not only help you to view your problems differently, but will train your mind to become more flexible, more creative and better able to deal with problems in the future.

Unlike other 'change your life' books, which require readers to work through a plan or programme from start to finish, only for the book to get forgotten or discarded, I'm going to recommend that you keep this book as a reference guide for the rest of your life. Whether you are young or old, already successful or waiting to become successful, there is something in this book that can help you and, such is the unpredictability of life, you'll never quite know when you might need it again.

2

NLP – What's It All About?

How it Began

Neuro-Linguistic Programming came into being in the early 1970s in California. Richard Bandler, a master's level student of Information Sciences and Mathematics, joined forces with Dr John Grinder, a Professor of Linguistics. At that time developments were already being made in the study of neuro-linguistics and how the use of language can influence the workings of the mind.

Bandler and Grinder became fascinated by the work of three highly successful psychotherapists – Fritz Perls (the founder of Gestalt Therapy), Virginia Satir (developer of Family Therapy) and Milton Erickson (Clinical Hypnotherapist) – whose words and suggestions had a direct impact on their patients' recovery.

They studied the strategies and language patterns used by these therapists to see if it was possible to identify what made them the best in their field. Bandler's mathematical and computer-programming skills were combined with Grinder's expertise in linguistics and they went on to 'code' this success formula. Not only did they discover that it was possible to create formulas for human behaviour, but that it was possible for others to replicate them and achieve similar success. Their creation of the methodology that is today known as NLP has made a significant contribution to our understanding of the workings of the human mind.

Despite its complicated-sounding name, NLP is really quite simple, and understanding the principles helps us to understand how our minds work – how information is absorbed by our brains and converted into thoughts and feelings that affect our behaviour. Since those early days, NLP has continued to be refined and developed by a vast array of individuals and is widely used in the fields of communication, commerce, personal development, psychotherapy, education and medicine. Bandler and Grinder continue to be actively involved and, although now working apart, develop and add new ideas on an ongoing basis.

More recently, Paul McKenna has been highly successful at introducing NLP to the general public through his popular series of self-help books which have sold millions of copies around the world.

NLP is becoming recognised as one of the most effective psychological methods. Put simply, NLP deals with what we think, what we say and what we do and is viewed as one of the most sophisticated and quickest methods of bringing about changes in people's lives.

Using Your Imagination

Every man-made item you see around you right now started off as an idea in someone's imagination. The clothes you wear, the meals you eat, the furniture you use, the streets you walk along and the car you drive all started off as an image or picture in someone's mind.

In order to 'create' your life on a conscious level, it has to start off in the same way – in your imagination. Having the ability to dream and imagine means having the power not only to design your life (and design it well) but also test it out and mentally rehearse it too, making sure it's just right for you, before going off and doing it for real. Indeed, it was Einstein who claimed that imagination is more important than knowledge.

NLP can teach you how to use your imagination in a positive way to improve your performance in almost anything. From top sports people to trainee pilots, it has now been demonstrated that 'mental rehearsal' in your imagination is the 'difference that can make a difference' and produce outstanding results.

To help this process along, NLP uses what are referred to as 'hypnotic trance-like states', which allow you to deliberately daydream in your subconscious mind. We've all drifted into daydreamy states – perhaps in front of the TV or on a long journey – and when we're in this hypnotic state, it can be said that our subconscious minds, rather than our conscious minds, are doing the thinking for us.

If you've ever felt 'in two minds' about something, it's because two minds is exactly what you have. Your conscious mind can think about the past, present and future, and it's the bit that reminds you to make that phone call or buy a loaf of bread.

The subconscious mind, far from being an old filing cabinet, is actually more like the motor or engine that drives you. Having been programmed from childhood by your environment and the experiences you've had, it stores all your habits and behaviours and acts like your personal automatic pilot. We all have a subconscious, but each person's is unique to them. However, the subconscious mind does much more than simply 'remember' the constant repetition of actions, habits, thoughts and ideas that go into it. This barrage of information actually 'creates' the subconscious mind – and so, creates you.

Most of us have driven a car, reached our destinations and worried that we couldn't remember a thing about the journey. You can worry no more, for your subconscious mind did the driving for you (remember how you programmed it with all those driving lessons?), leaving your conscious mind free to think about all sorts of other things. Your subconscious mind operated on autopilot whilst your conscious mind was set to manual.

This clever system of ours can sometimes be our downfall, especially when we're attempting to make big changes in our lives. Not all of the patterns of behaviour stored in the subconscious mind are helpful or useful – it's possible to pick things up without even realising it, for example phobias or anxieties and habits such as overeating or smoking.

It can sometimes feel a struggle, as the conscious and subconscious minds find themselves in conflict and it's why something like dieting can be very difficult. When you consciously try to make changes using brute force or will-power, an internal struggle takes place, as the subconscious mind continues to operate on autopilot.

It doesn't matter how much you try to cajole or bully your conscious mind into following a weight-loss regime: it's the patterns of behaviour that you've previously programmed into the subconscious mind that are running the show. The only sure way to succeed is to literally 're-program' your mind with more useful behaviours.

Drifting into a daydreamy 'trance state' allows your conscious mind to switch off, leaving your subconscious mind much easier to access. It's perfectly natural and something we all do several times a day.

In fact, there are times when our minds work best when we're not thinking too consciously. Have you ever had your mind go blank when asked for a simple piece of information, like your telephone number? If you 'think' about it too much, you can't remember it. But if you relax and do it without think-ing, the number comes easily out of your mouth. It's imprinted on your subconscious mind, but your conscious mind can sometimes find it a struggle to recall because it's busy think-ing about other things. And how many of us know people who claim they can write essays or articles better when they're drunk? Again, their subconscious mind is doing the work for them.

The subconscious part of your mind is, therefore, the best place to take those first few steps towards making any changes you'd like to see in your life, and NLP can make this whole process so much easier for you. It enables you to understand what makes you tick – how you think and make sense of the world – and there are many techniques which can easily change the 'programming' that lets you down, and turn it into successful patterns of behaviour. Rather than living your life accidentally, you can take charge of it and design it to look like the kind of life you'd like to have.

NLP and Hypnosis

Because a proportion of the work of NLP is carried out in the subconscious mind through trance-like states or hypnosis, many people ask about the differences between NLP and hypnotherapy.

Whereas hypnotherapy is a form of psychotherapy (where one examines one's life by relating the present to events that happened in the past) combined with hypnotic trance states, NLP is not used in the same therapeutic way. It's not unusual for conventional psychotherapy to take many months if not years to help people find a resolution to their problems, whereas the effects and benefits of NLP can be felt after just a couple of sessions.

NLP is more concerned with creating strategies for building success in the future and, whilst the past may relevant, it isn't regarded in the same way. Just because you've always done things in certain ways, it doesn't mean you have to continue to do them in that way. What's more important than your distant past is how you do things here and now in the present and how you would like to have them happening in the future.

Understanding what strategies your mind is running and how they can be changed is what NLP focuses on.

In fact, in order to become successful at using NLP, it is preferable not to spend too much time revisiting the past. Repeatedly replaying past memories and bad experiences only entrenches those unwanted patterns of behaviour more deeply. It's more helpful to put the emphasis on the future and how one would like things to be.

Sessions can be completely 'content-free', which means all the practitioner needs to know is what the problem is right now and what the goal or aim is for the future. Certain problems benefit from this 'brief' approach – for example, fear of flying. If a person has had a bad experience on an aeroplane in the past, talking it through again and again can reinforce the idea in the client's mind that flying is stressful, rather than taking the bad feelings away. An NLP practitioner would focus more on the mechanics of the problem – on what the client sees, hears and feels in their body – and set about making changes. A trance-like state would then be induced to enable the client to experience a pleasant, enjoyable flight in their mind, before going on to do it for real.

Whilst NLP practitioners can guide people into relaxed, trance-like states through their words, they have no magic powers. 'Under hypnosis', people are completely in control of their situation and the feeling is not unlike that of dozing off in front of the TV. As the chatter of the conscious mind is switched off, the subconscious mind is free and open to explore and take on new ideas.

For example, if you found yourself lacking in motivation to start exercising, a health professional could talk to you about the benefits, but the likelihood is that your conscious mind would already start creating excuses – not enough time, too expensive, too exhausting – and you would have to battle against those feelings.

If, on the other hand, a therapist relaxed you into a trance-like state to switch off your conscious mind and made positive suggestions to your subconscious mind instead, you would find yourself automatically somehow feeling that exercise would be a good idea. It would seem a more natural thing for you to do, as your mind readily accepted the suggestion, especially if you had already visualised yourself exercising happily during the trance.

Some people expect to be completely unconscious in trance states, but this is simply not the case and you are safe and completely in control throughout. If the room you were sitting in suddenly caught fire, trust me – you'd be out of your chair like a shot and straight out of the door. You certainly wouldn't need someone to come along and slap your face to bring you round.

Hypnosis is similar to meditation – however, the aim with meditation is to create a specific state on the inside. During hypnosis, suggestions offered by the therapist are designed to create some form of change on the outside, after the session.

The Secrets of Stage Hypnosis

Many people are scared of hypnosis, but they don't know why. Often this is based on what they have seen of stage shows as they wonder if they too will end up performing a silly walk and clucking like a chicken.

There are number of components to a stage show that make it seem magical. To begin with, there is the expectation of the audience, which influences their behaviour. They already know that some of them will be selected to behave in an extraordinary manner and this suggestion alone is enough to trigger off the exhibitionist tendencies that some of them have, especially if fuelled by alcoholic drinks beforehand.

There are many suggestibility tests that can be done on an audience: simple things such as asking people to stretch their hands out in front of them and close their eyes as they imagine a strong glue being applied to their palms. Then they are asked to stick their palms together with the suggestion being given that this is ultra-strong glue and they will struggle to release their hands. The people that follow this instruction and do indeed find themselves unable to separate their hands are deemed highly suggestible and perfect for a stage performance. They can be selected and seated together.

It's usual then for the stage hypnotist to ask for volunteers from this part of the audience. Those who put their hands up quickly will be chosen. Those who hesitate are rejected.

Further tests are placed in the participants' way. The hypnotist could have a row of chairs placed on the stage – let's say he has nine chairs. He could then select ten people from the volunteers who raised their hands quickly to come up and take a seat. As there's one chair short, the participant who is the slowest to respond will be without a chair and therefore eliminated. The hypnotist is seeking super-keen people.

With nine people seated on the chairs, he could ask them all to stand up and then to sit down again. The slowest to sit down can be eliminated again. At this stage, he may even reduce the group to just four or five people. He's looking for people who carry out his instructions immediately, without giving them any thought.

They'll each be asked to stand up and go through a few ridiculous exercises with him in front of the audience. He'll be monitoring how they respond to the audience's cheers of encouragement. Those who let themselves go and clearly enjoy putting on a performance will get to stay with him, whilst the others will be sent back to their seats.

This process of elimination could take a whole hour, by which time the last participant left on stage with the hypnotist is the most compliant along with having strong exhibitionist tendencies – adrenaline-fuelled, pumped up and ready to perform. The person is then able to behave as ridiculously as he chooses, safe in the knowledge that he can hand over

Remember This

NLP for Greater Success:

Whilst NLP is often put to use to solve problems, it isn't necessary to have any kind of problem at all in order to make good use of it. The techniques and strategies of NLP can be used to build on existing successes and it's regularly applied across all sorts of contexts: business applications, leadership, persuasion, sales, management, team-building, health, sports and relationships. Many people use it to become successful and then use it again to double that success, as they focus on what works in their life rather than on what doesn't.

the responsibility for his outrageous actions to the hypnotist. And at the end of it all, he can claim he can't remember a thing and so is blameless.

A truly hypnotised person would not be able to perform and dance around on stage, as the sign of a deep trance is actually complete stillness. Even when we are asleep, it's common to fidget and move around, but a deliberately induced hypnotic state is an altogether much calmer place to be.

You can rest assured that a 'stage show' is just that – a stage show.

3

Making Sense of It All

Did you know it's estimated that our nervous systems receive around two million bits of information about what is happening around us, every second of the day?

With so much information bombarding our minds, we quickly filter or condense it down into about seven bits of information that are more manageable. In order to do this we make **deletions, distortions** and **generalisations**. Let's look at these in a bit more detail:

- **Deletions**: We automatically have to delete some of the information we receive because there's simply too much of it so we *chunk it down* into a more manageable size. Because this can be a fairly random process, it's possible to throw away vital pieces of information without realising it.

- **Distortions**: We can make things seem better or worse than they really are as we make the information we receive compatible with our perceptions. In other words, it's not uncommon for our minds to have an idea and then seek out evidence to support it. For example: if you feel there are a lot of red cars on the road, it's very likely that red cars will 'pop out' at you as you drive along, supporting the notion.

- **Generalisations**: It's simply not possible to re-learn something every time we do it, so our minds make generalisations to speed things up for us. For example: if you learnt how to ride a bike, you can transfer that skill to all bikes, making the generalisation that they pretty much all work in the same way. This can cause a problem in other areas, e.g. developing a phobia of *all* dentists because you had a bad experience with just one.

The shrunken-down piece of incoming information (after you've deleted, distorted and generalised) becomes your **internal representation.**

Added to this cocktail of sensory information is the individual 'spin' we'll each put on what we witness. This spin will again vary enormously depending on our **beliefs, values** and **past experiences**.

The phrase 'Neuro-Linguistic Programming', while sometimes dismissed as a ridiculous title, actually describes perfectly this relationship between incoming information and outgoing behaviour:

- **Neuro** relates to your neurological processes (sensory input that's distorted, deleted and generalised, topped off with the personal 'spin' of beliefs, values and experiences).

- **Linguistic** refers to the words and language used – be they our own, other people's or what is around us in the environment, e.g. in advertising or on television, that profoundly affect our thinking and influence our behaviour.

- **Programming** refers to the Neuro-Linguistic input into our thoughts, feelings and behaviour and the results that it gives us.

Discovering how our neurological processes work in this way is perhaps NLP's greatest contribution to the field of psychology. It provides us with the means to understand how our minds 'code' information and how that information is represented throughout our bodies.

Downloading Sensory Information

As we've already seen, we download information from the events that happen around us through our senses or – as they are often referred to in NLP – **modalities**.

The two million bits of information that our nervous systems get bombarded with each second of the day get absorbed through our five senses: sight (visual), hearing (auditory), touch (kinaesthetic), smell (olfactory) and taste (gustatory), and then we code them.

In NLP, most emphasis is placed on the visual, auditory and kinaesthetic senses since they're the ones that we rely on most throughout the day. Our thoughts are a combination of pictures, sounds and feelings.

Visual: As well as actually seeing things around you with your eyes, you're also imagining pictures in your mind. As you think and speak you're constantly making pictures. They flash through your mind so quickly you may not even notice them, but identifying how and where you make your pictures can open up a whole new world for you.

Exercise: Making Pictures

To get your mind used to noticing how you construct these mind pictures, keeping your eyes open, think about the following objects, spending a few moments on each:

- a cat
- a baby
- an ice-cream.

Not all our pictures are made in the same way. Some are bright and colourful, others dim and fuzzy. Some are still images, just like photographs, and in others there's movement – a bit like watching a movie. Perhaps you'll see yourself in *outside* some of these pictures, so you'll be **dissociated**, and sometimes you'll feel as if you are actually in the picture and taking part – **associated**. We also make our pictures in different places depending on the emotion attached to the thought.

If I ask you to think about the capital of France and say its name out loud whilst imagining going on a trip there, you'll see what I mean. Some people will see a quick flash of the Eiffel Tower when they answer. Others will see the word itself, or the French flag or perhaps a Métro sign. All throughout the day, your mind is doing this, whether you're thinking about phoning a friend or what you need to buy from the shops today.

Test it out again – what did you eat for breakfast this morning? Even if the answer is 'nothing', you will nevertheless have caught a glimpse in your mind of where you were first thing this morning.

As we think and speak, our minds our constantly making pictures, even if we're not aware of it. These can have an enormous effect not only on our feelings but also on our behaviour and the results we get.

Humans are naturally goal-driven: it's our survival mechanism, what keeps us alive, forever moving forward and seeking food. And the curious thing is that our bodies automatically take the pictures in our minds as an instruction on what to do next. We are magnetically drawn towards getting what we can visualise.

Which is why negative thoughts can hold us back. No one ever visualised themselves failing and then surprised themselves by succeeding.

Using NLP enables you not only to notice the pictures that you make in your mind – good or bad – but also to change them or play around a little with them.

Changing the pictures in your mind will also change your feelings, because your body is always responding to the thoughts inside your mind. Which is why relaxation sessions always invite you to 'empty the contents of your mind', for with a relaxed mind, you'll easily have a relaxed body.

The human nervous system can't tell the difference between a real and imagined experience – which is why watching scary movies can make our hearts pound and our hands sweat. Despite the fact that you know it's only make-believe, your body will respond to the pictures it's looking at.

Close your eyes and dream of a nice, sunny, relaxing beach and your body will start to feel calmer.

Auditory: Not only are you constantly hearing the sounds around you, but you're also hearing the sounds you make inside your head all day long, whether you're playing a piece of music to yourself or listening to your inner voice, your 'internal dialogue'.

It's not unusual for people to completely lose touch with their internal dialogue. Some will insist that they have no internal dialogue whatsoever. It's there, of course, but in the busyness of life it can go unnoticed. Just stop right now and ask yourself (but not out loud) 'Where is my internal dialogue?' and you'll find it.

In fact, you not only have an inner voice that talks to you all day long, but you've got several. There's a happy, upbeat one and a miserable, negative one. There's one, or even a few, that don't sound anything like you at all – because they sound like other people. Your mother or father maybe, a critical teacher from schooldays gone by – a whole cast of extras living inside your head, just longing to have a conversation with you, or tell you what to do!

And what's more, they don't all live in the same place. Some live on the top of your head; others inside your mouth; there's one in your left ear and another in your right. And quite a nice, friendly one that sits inside your chest. Different voices live in different places, and learning where yours live and discovering how they sound is going to bring you one step closer to being more in control of them and the kind of things they say. Our words, and those used by other people, create the pictures in our minds – pictures that make us think and behave in certain ways.

Kinaesthetic: Think of all the sensations and feelings we experience on a regular basis – feelings of butterflies in the stomach; anxiety in the legs, arms or hands; feelings of confidence and excitement; sadness, disappointment and heaviness in our hearts. Because of our body's ability to habituate, we know that in order to keep feeling those feelings on the inside, they have to keep moving. Because quite simply, if they were to keep still we'd stop feeling them.

Imagine me stamping on your foot right now. It would most probably hurt and you probably wouldn't be very happy. If I repeated it over and over again, it would continue to hurt and you'd continue to be unhappy.

But if I were to press my foot down hard on yours, and just keep it there, initially you would feel pain but after a few moments you'd get used to the feeling and, guess what, you'd kind of stop feeling it. Your body would habituate to the pressure of my foot. Our bodies do this all the time in response to all sorts of things.

Can you remember the last time you jumped into a cold swimming pool? You soon got used to the temperature of the water and it stopped feeling so cold to you.

This kind of habituation can happen not only on the outside of our bodies but also on the inside. Learning how to keep feelings inside your body completely still or moving in a different direction will enable you to change the way you feel. You'll be able to take control and turn anxiety and bad feelings right the way down, and also be able to increase good feelings inside your body.

Primary Systems

We all know someone who just seems to have 'an eye for colour' or 'an ear for music', as the information absorbed by their senses is not equally distributed. People's occupations or hobbies – e.g. photography, cooking, music or gymnastics – often indicate if they have a **preferred system**. But it's also possible to detect their preferred system through their conversation, for their vocabulary will give it away.

People with a strong visual sense will often use phrases such as 'see the bigger picture', 'light at the end of the tunnel' or 'blue-sky thinking'. Those more auditorially inclined will tell you that they 'hear what you're saying' and that it 'sounds good'. A more kinaesthetic person might say, 'I feel as if I have the weight of the world on my shoulders', 'that's a bit deep for me' or ask you to 'run that past me again'.

For each of the five senses or sensory modalities, there are finer distinctions or qualities known as **submodalities**. These submodalities are the way we code and make up the structure of our internal experience.

Exercise: Do You Have a Preferred System?

Find out how you make your pictures. Take a couple of moments to think about the last holiday you took. Remember where you went and who with. Notice what you notice.

I wonder what it was about this holiday that you recalled the most? Did you bring to mind an image of the sights you saw – a beach or a city perhaps? Or the sounds – other people's voices, a special piece of music, or seagulls? Or perhaps your memory was a kinaesthetic one which gave you a feeling of excitement, or even nausea as you remembered an unpleasant meal?

What worked best for you? What made you feel good?

Your Visual Submodalities: Answer the following questions to discover the submodalities of that holiday picture of yours from the above exercise.

Location:	Where is that picture – is it in front of you or to one side?
	Can you point to it?
	Is it close to you or far away?
Colour:	Is it in colour?
	Or black and white?
Brightness:	Is the picture bright or is it dull?
Associated/ Dissociated:	Do you feel as if you are in the picture? Or are you looking at yourself in the image?
Size:	Is the picture big or small?
Still or movie?:	Is the picture still like a photograph? Or is it more like a movie?

Shape:	Square, round or rectangular?
Border:	Does the picture feel as if it has a frame around it?
	Or are there no borders as it fades away?
Focus:	Is it sharply in focus or is it fuzzy?

Your Auditory Submodalities: Just as the pictures in your head have these qualities, so too do the sounds you hear.

Location:	Where do you hear the sounds you're hearing?
	Inside your head?
	Or somewhere else – chest, throat or above your head?
	Is it to the left of your ear?
	Or the right side?
Words or sounds:	If you can hear words, can you recognise the voice?
	Is it yours or someone else's?
	What sounds can you hear?
Volume:	Is it loud or soft?
Tone:	What tone does the voice you hear have?
Mono or stereo:	Do you hear the sound on one side of your head, or both?
Tune/rhythm:	Does the sound have a tune or rhythm?

Your Kinaesthetic Submodalities: It's also possible to gain more information about your feelings. Perhaps you were able to notice which aspects of that particular memory made you feel good and which ones didn't.

Location: Where are you feeling those feelings in your body?

Can you point to the place?

Pressure: Does the feeling exert a pressure?

Size: Can you say whether it's small or big?

Shape: Does the feeling have a shape?

Colour: Could you give it a colour?

Intensity: Is it strong or weak?

Temperature: Does it feel hot, warm or cold?

4

Gaining Control of Your Mind

Rather than simply accepting the pictures that come into our minds, it's possible to gain more control over the way they look by changing the submodalities. The best way to understand how these submodalities can make a difference to your thoughts is to play around with them. It's a bit like having your own personal remote control.

Exercise: Playing with Pictures

Take your time with this exercise, pausing in between each of the steps. You may find it easier to do this with a friend or colleague.

1. Let's conjure up a new image. Think of a happy time – a party or event perhaps, or a time when you received a compliment or praise.
2. Become aware of the picture your mind is creating.
3. Is it in colour or black and white?
4. Make it colourful, turning up the colours brighter, bolder, stronger.

5. Notice how it changes your feelings.

6. And now, drain the colours out, turning the picture into black and white.

7. Notice the difference it makes.

8. And then turn them back into bright, bold colours once more.

9. Then move the picture around – take it far, far away, making it smaller.

10. And then bring it back, closer to you. Bring it right up in front of you.

11. Are there any sounds in your memory? The sound of other people's voices perhaps?

12. Turn the volume up . . . And now turn it up again . . . really loud.

13. Now make it quieter . . . Turn the volume right down or even completely off.

14. And raise it again so you can clearly hear all the sounds once more.

15. If you are 'dissociated' (i.e. you can see your whole body moving around in this memory) make yourself 'associated' (insert yourself into the picture so you feel as if you're there once more, experiencing things as you did before).

16. If your picture is a 'still', how about making it into a movie? Have everyone moving around.

17. And then freeze it once more – leaving it right up close to you, colours bright and bold, sounds up high.

18. And notice your feelings.

19. Can you point to the picture? Is it right in front of you, or slightly to one side?

Now that you've played around with that image, have a think about whether anything particularly struck you. Which changes amplified the good feelings in that memory and which changes reduced them?

Remember, once you've discovered how the construction of your thoughts, in pictures, words and feelings, affects your mood and behaviour, you'll be holding a very valuable key which will give you greater power over your life than you've ever had before. You'll be able to transfer this 'code' to other thoughts and ideas, and making your pictures match in terms of size, shape, colours, proximity and sounds will generate more good feelings for you.

You'll be able to make sad or unhappy thoughts go away, melt anxiety, download motivation or crank up your happiness levels whenever you need to.

Getting Rid of Bad Pictures

If I came to your house tonight, switched on your TV and fiddled with the channels to find a programme featuring you experiencing the biggest and worst problem in your life, would you sit down and watch it? Would you leave it on so every time you came home you had a great, big reminder of what it is you'd rather forget?

'Of course not' is the answer most people would give. But in reality, this is what most of us do. We store pictures in our minds of precisely all the things that upset us the most. Some of us even create movies out of them – in glorious Technicolor – and re-live the horrific moments of our lives over and over. And then we wonder why we feel so bad.

The good news is there's a very simple way of banishing these thoughts and pictures just by using the 'remote control' for your mind. Try this simple technique.

Exercise: Reducing Bad Feelings

If this is your first time, pick an example that is not too traumatic – once you get the hang of it, you can work with more serious issues.

Can you think of a minor disagreement that you had recently? Are you playing it over and over in your mind? Remember my comment about your TV – why do you keep looking at it and why are you replaying it, if it does not make you feel good?

1. Take yourself back to that irritating moment.
2. Notice where the picture is positioned.
3. Is it in colour or black and white?
4. Are there any sounds?
5. And what about the size?
6. Does it have a border around it?

OK – let's change pictures:

1. If it is in colour, turn the picture into black and white.
2. Next, shrink the picture down.
3. Turn the volume down so you can no longer hear those voices.
4. Move that picture further and further away.
5. Shrink it right down into a dot.

6. And now imagine taking a paintbrush and painting it white.
7. Whiten it out.
8. And notice how it changes your feelings.

Always remember that good pictures in our minds create good feelings and bad pictures create bad feelings. Pictures that are closer and more colourful intensify the feelings. So this is good news for the memories that you'd like to savour. And pictures with the colours drained out of them and positioned far away will have far less intensity and, as such, will automatically have less of an impact on your feelings.

Our **internal representations** (or pictures) affect the way we feel – in NLP terms we call this our **state**. Our state has a direct effect on our physiology, which is why happy people have a much more upright posture and depressed people slouch downwards. Internal representations, state and physiology are interlinked and affect each other. This is why lucky people seem to attract more luck and unhappy people can attract more problems – your state has an influence on what happens around you.

The Eyes Have It

Depending on the type of thoughts we are having, our eyes move around and we look in different directions.

Richard Bandler and John Grinder first discovered this when giving lectures to audiences of around 300 people. They would ask the audience a specific question and then see all the people's eyes moving up and across to the left as they pondered an answer. They would then ask another question and, this time, see everyone's eyes looking up and across to the right. Because so many people were looking in the same direction at the same time, in response to a specific question, they realised that there had to be a reason for this – it was much more than just a coincidence.

One of the best ways to see this in action is to watch a television programme such as *Mastermind*. Watch the contestants' eyes as they move up in response to a question. As they try to retrieve the answer, you'll be able to see their gaze move in different directions.

The reason for this is that the human eye is connected to the brain by a set of muscles – as your mind begins to sort through its thoughts and starts accessing different parts of the brain, your eye muscles get tugged along in the same direction.

This activity gives us massive clues about what is going on inside people's minds and it's even possible to detect if someone is lying or telling the truth.

Exercise: Feel Your Gaze Move

- Think about what you had for lunch yesterday.

And now:

- Think about what you might be eating for tomorrow's lunch.

And again:

- Think about where you went on holiday last year.

And now:

- Think about where you might go on holiday next year.

You may have felt your gaze move in different directions in response to these statements. In each example, the first instruction asked you to retrieve a memory (visual remembered), and the second instruction asked you to imagine what you might be doing in the future (visual constructed). And most likely, your eyes were looking up towards the ceiling. You were accessing different sorts of pictures and your eye movements gave a clue to this.

When you think about sounds rather than pictures, your eyes will be moving to the left and right in line with your ears. Think about a favourite piece of music, for example. Now imagine an unusual sound, such as a hyena laughing perhaps.

If you're talking to yourself, you'll probably find your eyes moving to the left, and they'll point downwards as you listen to your internal dialogue.

When your eyes look down and to the right, you'll tend to be accessing the 'feeling' part of your mind.

Our eye movements correspond with the different representational systems (visual, auditory, kinaesthetic) we have.

Identifying how and where your eyes move will enable you to have more control over your thoughts and the outcomes of those thoughts.

Accessing Cues: The table below shows how the majority of us process information in relation to our eye movements. However, in a small percentage of the population, including around half of all left-handers, this is reversed. So their eye movements would be a mirror image of what is shown here.

Pattern	Eyes Move To	Reason
Visual constructed	Top right	Seeing new or different images
Visual remembered	Top left	Seeing images seen before
Visual	Blank stare ahead	Either new or old images
Auditory constructed	Centre right	Hearing new or different sounds
Auditory remembered	Centre left	Remembering sounds
Auditory internal dialogue	Bottom left	Talking to yourself
Kinaesthetic	Bottom right	Feelings, emotion, touch

While this body language gives us wonderful clues about what's going through other people's minds, I get more excited about the additional control you can gain over your own mind.

Exercise: Likes and Dislikes

1. Think of someone you love and adore. Get that picture nice and strong by turning up the colours.
2. Think of someone you dislike, the more the better. Think of someone on TV or in the movies if you can't immediately think of a person you know personally. Become aware of where you are seeing these pictures.
3. What's your favourite food – something you really like? Think of it and make that picture big and strong.
4. Think of a food that you dislike – one that you wouldn't touch in a million years.
5. Think of a car you'd love to drive. What's your favourite make? And what colour would you have it in?
6. Now think of a car you wouldn't be seen dead in.

Now compare your images. Like most people you probably discovered that you make pictures of things you like on one side and that all those pictures of things you dislike popped up on the other side. This is very valuable information for you.

You have now identified the place where you see pictures of things you strongly like. And you also have identified the place where you see pictures of things you strongly dislike.

Think of the advantages. Next time you're craving some chocolate biscuits, locate the picture that pops into your mind and, literally, move it across to the place where you made pictures of foods you disliked. And notice how it changes your feelings!

Next time you have a task to do (like filling in that tax return) and you find yourself struggling to motivate yourself – stop and think. What does motivate you? Could you make a good picture of it? And then make a picture of your tax return. Are they in the same place? If not, move your 'tax return picture' across to the place where you make your 'motivated pictures'. And notice how it changes your feelings.

And what about all those times when you'd like to embark on something new, but you just don't quite believe you're capable of doing it. (Someone told you that, right?) Then think of something you do believe strongly in – the number of brothers or sisters you have, for example; what you will be doing tomorrow – you believe that there will be a tomorrow, don't you? And notice where you make those pictures. And then compare that place to the place where you made the picture that made you wobble with doubt. Are they in the same place? Most likely not – move the picture across and enjoy the feelings of strong belief filter through your body.

Mind Your Language

Not only do our feelings affect the pictures we create in our minds, but so do the words we hear – either those spoken by someone else or the ones we say to ourselves that make up our internal dialogue.

If you often find yourself struggling to achieve your goals, it's worth checking the words you use when you speak to yourself.

Think of something you've had on your 'to do' list for quite a while. Make a sentence out of it, beginning with the words below:

I must
I should
I ought to
I may
I might
I could
I'll try

'I must sort out the cupboards' will not only give you a negative feeling, but will also be creating a picture in your mind that suggests an uphill struggle. Perhaps you'll get a picture of messy cupboards in your mind.

Whereas 'I'm going to sort out the cupboards on Tuesday' puts a completely different complexion on the matter. Those words are more likely to produce a picture of clean and tidy cupboards in your mind.

'I ought to walk the dog' implies that it's something that

you've been putting off doing. The picture that springs to mind might be one of an unwalked dog looking forlorn.

Whereas 'I will walk the dog this morning' creates a momentum and might conjure up an image of you and your dog striding along in the fresh air.

Notice too that I added a couple of extra words second time around – 'on Tuesday' and 'this morning'. Being more specific about your commitment means you are more likely to do it.

Remember, human beings are driven by the images created in their minds – your body will always be driven to doing what it sees itself doing in your imagination. Positive pictures create positive results and negative ones are more likely to hold you back.

Exercise: Trying

Follow this exercise to discover how negative pictures can hold you back. And why not test it out on a friend or colleague? Ask them to close their eyes and follow your instructions.

1. Close your eyes and see in your imagination a door.
2. Notice the colour of the door and say the colour out loud.
3. Open the door.
4. When you have opened the door, open your eyes. Pause.
5. Close your eyes again and see in your imagination another door.

6. Notice the colour of the door and say the colour out loud.
7. Now this time, try to open the door. Pause.
8. Open your eyes and come back into this room.
9. What difference did you find between the first door and the second door?

Were the doors the same colour, or different? Did they have handles, locks or bolts? Were the handles on the same side? Did the doors open slowly or quickly?

As you'll discover, when you use the word 'try' you will either find it difficult or you will not be able to do it at all. It's quite incredible how such a small word can have such a big impact, but it does – by automatically suggesting that whatever it is you're planning to do, you're going to struggle with it.

This is an interesting exercise and will probably make you think back to your schooldays. How many times did someone say to you 'as long as you *try*, that's all that matters', '*try* your best', 'just *try* and have a go' or, best of all, '*try your hardest*!' Twice in one sentence, it has been suggested to you that you're going to struggle.

How different would the results have been if you had been given positive directions rather than those negative ones that held you back?

'What you see is what you get' is a phrase I often use with my clients, for our bodies act upon the 'instructions' we give them. They take their cue from the pictures we make in our imaginations and the words we use, as if they were magnetically drawn towards them.

It's why I teach my clients the importance of putting good pictures into their minds by focusing on what they do want, rather than on what they don't want. When I work with clients for weight loss, for example, I always instruct them to remember to think positively, rather than negatively. 'I don't want to look fat on the beach' becomes 'I want to look good in a bikini'.

Remember, your words will create a picture in your mind and your body will automatically spring into action to make it turn into a reality for you. Giving it positive instructions to follow is what will create positive pictures for you and good results will follow. Always focus on what you

Remember This

Remember how as a child you learned how to put jigsaw puzzles together by looking at the picture on the box? The picture was your guide and you gathered up the pieces of the puzzle and made it match the picture. Your mind works in exactly the same way. It will look at the picture you are showing it and then work hard to ensure that it makes your reality match that picture as closely as possible. Which is why if you want to lose weight, telling yourself that you 'want to start exercising' is going to be much more motivating than 'I want to stop eating chocolate'.

How many of us have had an embarrassing experience, say tripping up in public, and then discover that no matter how many times we say to ourselves, 'Got to be

careful, I don't want to trip, I mustn't trip', it feels as if we are magnetically drawn to doing precisely that. It doesn't matter that you've been able to walk without tripping thousands of times before; our desire to ensure that we don't make the same mistake twice can mean that we spend our time focusing on what we don't want.

do want to have happen, rather than on what you *don't*.

How many of us have witnessed young children being told, 'Don't touch the vase!', only to see them do exactly that? It's because there are no pictures for negative words like *don't, no, not, never,* so our minds can only make pictures from the remaining words – which are often what we don't want to have happen. The child could only make a picture from two of the words spoken, 'touch' and 'vase', so it's not surprising that his body took over and followed the instructions.

'Let's leave the room nice and tidy' will produce a different result from 'Don't leave your room in a mess'. 'Let's see if we can be early today' is much more likely to get a child putting their skates on than 'Don't be slow or we'll be late'.

5

S-T-R-E-T-C-H Your Mind

In this chapter, I'll be showing you how to use and exercise your mind in different ways. Just as you'd exercise your body and practise various skills to improve your physical perform-ance, so it's possible to give your mind the same treatment. Following the strategies here will help to programme your mind for success, enabling you to fix those irritating problems and make positive changes.

Make the Difference that Makes the Difference

Have you ever walked into a room of people and felt you could cut the atmosphere with a knife? You couldn't quite put your finger on it, but you could sense something was wrong. The micro-messages you were receiving indicated that all was not well.

And if you've ever had a new haircut, only to discover that your nearest and dearest notices nothing different about you, you'll know that not all of us notice the same things in the same way. Some of us notice far many more details than others.

Compare your 'clutter threshold' to that of the people you live with. Some of us can tolerate quite a messy environment whereas others need a spick-and-span, decluttered environment in order to feel relaxed. Teenagers are notorious for living quite happily in untidy bedrooms, much to their parents' dismay, and it has even been reported that men don't seem to 'see' dust!

As we've already discovered, your senses receive all the information from what's happening around you and deliver it to you ready to be filtered and interpreted by your mind.

Some people seem to pick up on every tiny detail and others prefer to see 'the bigger picture'.

What is it that you're not noticing that perhaps other, more successful, people are?

'What we see depends mainly on what we look for'
Sir John Lubbock

Over time, our senses get trained to seek out specific information and it's not uncommon to have one or two senses more dominant than the others.

Think of how a musician, an artist, a chef, an accountant and a tennis player would differ in their sensory acuity. All could be highly successful in their own right and highly tuned to seeking out certain bits of information. Over time, inevitably, the power of the senses they use less will start to fade.

We can get stuck in a rut in the way that we use our senses, which is why trying to solve a particular problem or achieve something new can seem to be a struggle if we continue to do things in the same way.

The good news is that no matter what age you are, it's never too late to refine your sensory acuity. And it's why people who lose a sense, such as their eyesight or hearing, often find their other senses becoming stronger.

It's possible to refine your sensory acuity by paying greater attention to the information you receive through your senses. The more you pay attention, the greater your ability to discriminate and the finer the details you can gather. Being successful is going to require you to be more observant and more self-aware than ever before.

How Will Refining My Sensory Acuity Help Me?: You'll start receiving important information that can:

- Enable you to become more creative

- Improve your problem-solving skills

- Enrich the pleasure you get in life

- Enhance your people skills

- Have you learning new things faster and more accurately

Tune into your sensory acuity when:

- You want to find out the difference that makes the difference

- You want more information than words are giving you

- Whenever you want to enjoy something more

- You are modelling someone (see 'Develop a Copycat Nature', p. 70)

The following exercises will help to refine your senses.

Exercise: Notice the Difference

Get into the habit of noticing more detail and of asking yourself what kind of detail is important – 'the difference that makes a difference'.

1. If someone appears confident, what is it about their demeanour that makes you feel this? The tone of their voice? Their posture or hand gestures?
2. If someone strikes you as being well-dressed, just what is it about their clothing, or their choice of clothing, that makes you think that?
3. How does a microwaved-from-frozen meal differ from one that has been freshly cooked?
4. Can you tell the difference between a cheap wine and vintage wine?
5. If you enjoy walking in the country, what exactly is it that you enjoy so much? Perhaps it's seeing the fields and trees and wildlife, or enjoying the changes of the seasons. Perhaps it's the feeling of walking in the fresh air or the rhythm of striding along. If you delight in what you see, is it the colour, the shapes, the variety that pleases you? What can you hear? What about smells? Can you taste anything? What are the micro-messages that you're picking up?

Exercise: Smell

You will need six dishes or plates, some loose-leaf tea, ground coffee and a selection of herbs and spices, e.g. rosemary, Chinese five spice, oregano and sage.

Place a small quantity of each ingredient into two of the dishes. Then place them at random on the table in front of you.

Wearing a blindfold, lift each dish, have a good smell and see if you can find its match, by smelling each of the other dishes. You can choose to make this exercise harder for yourself by choosing substances with similar smells.

Exercise: Touch

You will need a selection of fabrics, e.g. corduroy, silk, cotton, suede and linen. Ensure you have two pieces of each type of fabric.

Place them at random on the table in front of you. Then, wearing a blindfold once more, match the pieces by feeling the different textures.

You can make this exercise harder for yourself by choosing different grades of the same fabric, e.g. cotton in differing thread counts.

Exercise: Taste

Begin by eating your dinner wearing a blindfold. How does the taste differ from the other times you've eaten this meal? What new messages are you picking up? Does the food taste better or worse?

If you usually eat your meal in front of a TV or while reading a newspaper, you should be able to notice a major difference.

The next step is to gather a selection of foodstuffs with similar flavours, e.g. aniseed/liquorice, marjoram/oregano. Place each ingredient onto two plates and then lay your plates out randomly on the table in front of you.

Wearing a blindfold, match the ingredients by tasting them.

Alternatively, you could make this exercise trickier by asking a friend to give you some mystery foods to taste and identify.

Exercise: Visual

Exercise One: Collect leaves from the garden or park. Pick at least twenty different leaves. Now sort them into categories according to their shapes. How many different shapes can you identify? Are they all different? Which ones, regardless of size and colour, have the same shape?

Exercise Two: Take a few moments to look around the room. Notice everything in it that is green (for example). Now go out of the room and write down everything you saw of that colour. Come back into the room and compare.

You can make this exercise harder by working with a friend. Ask them to notice everything in the room that's *green* (for example). Once they have left the room, ask them to write down everything they saw that was *red* (i.e. choose a different colour from the one you asked them to notice). Go back into the room and compare.

Exercise: Auditory

Take a walk outside in a local park or through some woods. Listen out for birdsong. How many different varieties of song can you hear? Many varieties of birds will be living in the trees around you. If they all sound the same, you're missing something. Listen again.

So, having worked with each of your senses, what did you discover? How much valuable information did you miss? This is what your mind fails to absorb each and every minute of the day. Resolve to pick up on all extra information from now on.

These exercises will not only help you to refine your senses so you can sense more than other people, but you'll be able to discriminate and perceive 'the difference that makes a difference'.

Wear Another Man's Shoes

Imagine you are one of four witnesses to a road traffic accident: a motorcyclist has collided with a car at a busy junction. A police officer gathering evidence will undoubtedly end up with four different versions of the event. Each witness will have absorbed the details through their senses and then condensed or filtered the information in their minds. This shrunken down interpretation of the event becomes their internal representation.

However, internal representations can vary enormously from person to person. Not only do we all *delete, distort* and *generalise* in different ways, but our senses are not equally acute.

Added to this cocktail of sensory information is the individual 'spin' we'll each put on what we witness. This 'spin' again will vary enormously depending on our *beliefs, values* and *past experiences*. Even if we cannot consciously remember events from our childhoods, they will nevertheless have become 'imprinted' or tattooed upon our subconscious minds, creating reference points for us. Imagine that one of those people witnessing the accident was a road traffic police officer who dealt with accidents such as this most days of the week. And then imagine that another one of those people was a mother who had lost her 20-year-old son in a motorbike accident just last week. Same accident, but two completely different impressions and, as a result, two differing accounts.

It's not surprising to hear people say things like 'Get in the "real" world!' or 'What planet are you on?' as they struggle to understand that you might have a different point of view. The truth is there is no 'real' world, only our individual perceptions of it. Sometimes our perceptions will match other people's and other times they'll vary enormously.

A fundamental assumption of NLP is that we each have our own 'map of the world' and our backgrounds, culture, professional training and personal history will shape and form this map throughout our lives. Learning to use NLP helps us to deal with the fact that we each have different maps.

Learning how to see things from a different perspective or point of view will allow you to have greater flexibility and, like a muscle, this is something you can exercise and develop in many different ways.

In NLP we talk about taking different 'positions' to help us see things from a different perspective:

- 1st position: This is our own viewpoint and this is our starting point.

- 2nd position: This is the term used to describe the other's point of view.

- 3rd position: Here you are able to take a step back, detach and recognise both points of view.

It's really useful to be able to move around from one position to the next, as and when the situation demands it. Becoming more aware of these positions will enable you to handle situations more effectively and communicate better to resolve conflicts.

Getting stuck in one position can present problems. We can probably all think of people we know who operate from just one position. Generally speaking, people who live in the 1st position tend to have big egos and only see the world from their point of view.

Those spending most of their time in the 2nd position tend to be easily swayed with no real opinions of their own, always seeing things from others' points of view.

Exercise: Different Positions

James and Sarah had recently started living together – essentially they were very happy and things were going well. Both keen cooks, they enjoyed nothing more than a quiet night in as they tried out their favourite recipes on each other.

However, they quickly discovered that they had very different 'clutter thresholds'. Whilst James was organised and preferred the kitchen work surfaces to be completely clear and tidy, Sarah was a bit more relaxed in her approach and would prefer to have all the jars of ingredients and gadgets scattered around the kitchen.

One day, it was Sarah's turn to cook and she came home after a hard day at work to discover that James had packed all her things away and hidden them in cupboards – now she couldn't find a thing.

- 1st position: James
- 2nd position: Sarah
- 3rd position: fly on the wall

Put yourself into each of these positions and notice what thoughts and feelings come up.

And those only operating in the 3rd position can become detached observers of life, rather than participants.

Perceptual Positions in the Workplace: A commonly used strategy in the corporate world is actually named after Walt Disney, the Disney Strategy. People were often puzzled by his approach to developing creative ideas as he regularly used to shift position from one way of behaving to another. No sooner had he come up with an idea than he seemed to oppose it.

Exercise: Three Chairs

This exercise was developed by Robert Dilts, a key player in the NLP world, in 1988, and working through it will enable you to experience shifting through the positions more easily.

You will need three chairs, about four feet away from each other, set out in a triangle. Think of a situation you encountered recently with a friend, family member or work colleague where you both had different perspectives.

- 1st position: Sit in the first chair and experience that situation once more, through your own perspective. What are you thinking, feeling, hearing and saying to yourself once more as you look across to the second chair, which represents the other person? (If you find it easier, you can write your thoughts down on a piece of paper.)
- 2nd position: Now move to the second chair and pretend to be the other person. What experience are you having now – what are you thinking and feeling as you look across to the 'person' in the first chair? Speak out loud as if you really were this person.
- 3rd position: Now move across to the third chair and take a few moments to observe both 'people' in the other chairs. Think about how these two people have related to each other and to the situation. Take a look at the first chair and ask yourself what advice you could give.

If you still need to gain greater insight, you can repeat this exercise by sitting in each of the chairs again. Notice how you might feel differently about the original situation.

Robert Dilts analysed his behaviour and found it fell into three distinct elements. He gave each element a name: 'The Dreamer', 'The Realist' and 'The Critic'. This strategy is now well known and replicated in many commercial organisations as it aids brain-storming sessions and helps to turn creative ideas into reality.

But you can also use it in your personal life – if you come up with an idea and you're not sure whether it's a good one, enlist the help of a couple of friends and assign them their roles.

- **The Dreamer**: This role can be yours. Describe the idea in detail to the other participants. This can be your opportunity to embellish the idea and 'big it up', as you explore the different aspects of it.

- **The Realist**: This person's role is to take the idea and come up with the practical steps needed to turn it into a reality. Has anything been missed? What actions need to be taken and in what order?

- **The Critic:** As the name suggests, this person's role is to critically evaluate the likelihood of the project or idea succeeding.

Each stage should be explored thoroughly and once complete will have produced plenty of valuable information on which you can base your final decision.

Keep Your Glass Half Full

We're all familiar with advertisers and politicians putting a 'spin' on products and events to distort them to appear better than they really are. In NLP we do a similar thing and call it 'reframing'. Applying this same technique to events in your life so that you can view them in a different way will put you in a more resourceful state to solve problems and be creative.

'We're not retreating, we're just advancing in another direction.'
General George S. Patton

Exercise: Reframing
Read through these statements and see how the emphasis can be changed.

- I've just lost my job and I'm worried how I'll survive

can become:

- Losing my job means I'll be free to move to a new company and potentially increase my salary.

- It rained on holiday each day and we couldn't lie on the beach

can become:

- Because it rained on holiday, we found ourselves visiting interesting places and meeting more people.

- My car's broken down and will have to be in the garage for two weeks

can become:

- While my car's in the garage, I'll be able to walk to work and get that extra exercise I've been promising myself.

Now it's your turn. Write down three examples of bad news in your life (or someone else's) and reframe it to turn it into good news.

Acquiring the skill and flexibility to think creatively will enable you to tackle life's problems from a position of strength, rather than a position of weakness.

'There's no such thing as bad weather – only the wrong clothes'
Billy Connolly

In each of the cases, nothing has changed – the situation is as it is. But the important thing is that your perspective has changed to a positive one, enabling you to dream up solutions to your problems.

If you're feeling overwhelmed and deflated after losing your job, for example, your creativity will be stunted at exactly the time you'll be needing it the most. So using the art of 'reframing' doesn't mean you're viewing the world through rose-tinted specs; it helps you get back up on your feet again, ready to get going.

Get Along with Almost Anyone

We've all experienced that feeling of just seeming to 'click' with someone. Perhaps you can think of a few friends who you just seem to gel with. It's not uncommon for us to begin behaving the same way and even dressing in a similar way to our closest friends. Conversations flow easily as we adopt the same tone of voice or use of vocabulary and even our gestures seem to match and mirror theirs. We're on the same wavelength with these people and in NLP this is defined as 'rapport'.

However, I'm sure you can also think of a few people with whom you do not share such an easy relationship, or quite so much rapport. People at work, for example, or members of your extended family. Some things just seem to jar.

And what about meeting someone for the first time? New encounters can go one of two ways – you'll either get on like a house on fire and feel like you've known each other for years or it can feel a little awkward as you struggle to get a conversation going.

Just imagine how much easier life would be if all your interpersonal relationships were as comfortable as those with your best friends. What would you be able to achieve?

Refining your communication skills and building rapport is considered to be one of the pillars of NLP. For if you can instantly 'click' with people, just imagine how many doors could open for you and how many problems you'd be able to solve.

Studies have shown that communication is generally made up of 55 per cent body language, 38 per cent quality of voice and, rather worryingly, only 7 per cent actual words.

In almost every area of life we need to communicate with other people and the better you can become at falling in step with people quickly, the more you'll be able to achieve.

People tend to like each other, if they are like each other, but fortunately, this doesn't mean that you're going to have to actually like everyone. It's possible to be in rapport with someone and still disagree with them.

Having the ability to quickly gain rapport with someone will enable you to:

- Be more effective in interviews

- Be a more successful salesperson

- Be an effective negotiator

- Enjoy social situations more

- Enhance your friendships

- Have more success dating.

Gain rapport with someone by mirroring their behaviour in several key areas.

Posture and Movements: Do they have their legs crossed or their arms folded; are they leaning back or sitting forward; do they tilt their head to one side, stroke their chin or play with their hair?

Exercise: People-watching

1. Take up people-watching. Go to your local coffee bar and identify those people 'in rapport'. Watch their body language and their facial expressions. Can you see couples mirroring each other's movements? And who looks like they're not getting along? How can you tell?

2. Think about two people you know – one that you have obvious rapport with and another that you don't. What's similar about your body language, speech and tone of voice? And what's different? What could you change?
   • Breathing
   • Tone of voice
   • Speed of talking
   • Gestures: hand-waving, chin-stroking, playing with hair, raising eyebrows, smiling, scowling, pointing
   • Posture: formal, upright, laid-back, casual
   • Vocabulary, keywords and phrases

3. Put your observations into practice. Next time you're with someone, see if you can gain rapport by subtly mirroring them.

It's important to be very careful to be discreet about literally copying their movements or you could find them becoming upset if it's too obvious. That's why it's a good idea to start off slowly when you begin to practise. As a general rule, if the person you are matching shifts their position, leave about a thirty-second gap before adjusting yourself to match theirs.

Tone of voice: It's possible to easily fall into step with someone by simply matching the tonality of their voice. This is a particularly useful skill to adopt in telephone conversations when you cannot see the other person, and can prove invaluable if you have a job that entails a lot of telephone work – in a call centre, for example.

If someone begins to tell you a story in an excited voice, matching it will mean you come across as being equally excited by whatever it is they are telling you. Responding to their story in a slower, flatter-sounding voice could indicate to them that you are finding their story less exciting than they do. Demonstrating emotional rapport sends out a signal that you are sharing their experience and understand it.

And if you found yourself having to deal with an angry person (a complaining customer, for example), using a similarly outraged voice would indicate to them that you completely understand their feelings and would be feeling the same way if you were them. Responding to them with a much quieter and slower voice could make them even angrier.

Representational System: Become aware of whether the person you're matching has a preferred way of representing the world to themselves: are they more visual, auditory or kinaesthetic? The type of words they use when they're speaking to you will give you clues. You can quickly build rapport by using similar sorts of phrases.

This is where those phrases I pointed out earlier come into play – people with a visual preference tend to use phrases such as 'I see what you mean', 'seeing the bigger picture' or 'a sight for sore eyes'. Those with an auditory preference will be more likely to tell you that something 'strikes a chord', is 'clear as a bell' or is 'music to my ears'. And people with a preferred kinaesthetic representation will tell you that they 'need to get a grip on things' by 'taking things one step at a time' and will tell you that someone is a 'pain in the neck'. Notice the other person's favourite phrases and keywords and see if you can begin to match theirs, to get yourselves on the same wavelength.

Pacing and Leading: Once you've mastered the art of matching someone's voice, you'll quickly discover that it's possible to 'lead' them in a certain direction.

Begin by matching the pitch of the person's voice – this will make them feel as if they are being properly listened to. Continue to match them for about three or four minutes. And then gradually alter the tone and speed of your voice. At this point, you'll notice that the other person gradually starts matching your voice and as a result a significant change in their mood will occur.

This can work well for lifting the spirits of a person who is feeling down, diffusing anger in an irate person and increasing positivity in negative people.

Physical Rapport: It's possible to get more in rapport with someone by being aware of your physical relationship with them. For example, sitting opposite someone across a table can often mean that you see things differently. By moving to sit next to them, you'll be able to see things from the same perspective.

This can be particularly important in sales and business environments. Holding a meeting with your sales force sitting around a table can produce conflicting opinions. Rearranging the furniture to a 'theatre-style' layout will enable everyone to be facing the same way and quite literally have the same point of view.

Develop a Copycat Nature

It's not unusual to hear top sports people and other high achievers claim that they were influenced by a childhood hero and tried to be just like them. It's said that 'imitation is the sincerest form of flattery' and the NLP *modelling* process works in a similar way.

Modelling is often said to be at the heart of NLP – it's how Richard Bandler and John Grinder began their studies. They studied the behaviour and language patterns of experts in the field of psychological therapy and discovered that if they closely replicated their way of working, they too could achieve excellent results with patients.

They called this 'modelling' and it quickly became apparent that this could be applied to almost any kind of skill or technique.

Modelling is in fact a natural way of learning and it's a skill with which we are born. Humans can be seen as 'slow' in developmental terms – compare the eighteen months it takes us on average to learn how to walk with animals such as horses whose young spring up and walk within hours of being born. This 'delay' in our development is what enables us to be the superior of the species. We can adapt to our environments more readily – pick up a giraffe and place him in the North Pole and he will die. Whereas human beings have the ability to change and mould themselves to their surroundings.

As we get older, our patterns of behaviour become fixed through repetition and we forget that modelling is a good way of learning how to do something new or how to do something differently.

We become accustomed to the idea that we are good at some things and not others and are content to leave it there. How many of us limit ourselves with phrases such 'I'm useless at . . .', 'I'll never be any good at . . .','It's too late to change', 'You can't teach an old dog new tricks'?

NLP modelling is a more specific way of learning – for the natural modelling you did as a child was slightly more haphazard. The more you can spend time in the company of people who live the way you want to live, the more you can become like them. The more you can study and watch people who have the kind of skills you'd like to have, the more likely you are to get them.

If you don't know anyone who has the kind of skills you'd like to acquire, join groups and find appropriate mentors amongst them.

To successfully model someone you need to:

1. Identify the behaviour or skill that you'd like to adopt

2. Identify a peak performer in this area

3. Watch, study and notice – what is it that this person is doing that makes him the success that he or she is?

Exercise: The Coffee Shop

Take a trip to your local coffee shop and imagine you were starting work here as a barista, serving coffees to queues of eager customers.

If the manager of the shop took you into his office and talked you through the process of serving cups of coffee, you'd get an idea of what to do and might be able to do a pretty OK job.

But I'm sure you'll recognise that by standing behind the counter and watching one of the baristas demonstrate the process of dispensing ground coffee into a container, attaching it to the hot water outlet, steaming milk and adding a topping you'd be able to become much more proficient in a shorter space of time.

Test it out – next time you're in that coffee shop, watch the baristas at work. Do they all work in the same way? Or does one of them appear to be better at it than the others? What makes him that little bit better? Is he working faster? Can he pour a better cup of coffee? Does he have a better manner with the customers?

What is it that makes him that little bit better than the rest? If you were starting work at this coffee shop, which employee would you most like to model?

Modelling Excellence: When you first begin to consciously 'model' someone's behaviour, pick something straightforward and simple. You could copy someone's eating habits, for example.

1. If you were to eat as they do, how would you have to hold your knife and fork?

2. How much food would you have to pick up and put in each mouthful?

3. Do they take one item at a time?

4. Or do they enjoy merging their meat, potatoes and vegetables?

5. Do they chew their food thoroughly or do they shovel it down?

6. Do they leave something on their plate or do they clean it?

7. And how do they place their knife and fork on the plate when they have finished eating?

Imagine:
* How would a fussy eater who clearly wasn't enjoying his meal eat?

* And how would a hearty eater sitting down to his favourite meal eat?

If you were to model each of these eating habits, do you think it would change your experience of the meal? Would you enjoy one more than the other? You wouldn't just be copying the behaviour, you'd be able to change the experience.

Once you understand the behaviours and thinking patterns of other people you can begin to select those people who have achieved excellence in their field and start acting more like them.

Remember This

NLP Presupposition: *If one person can do something, we can all learn how to do it.*

Switch Your Feelings

Feelings, sensations and responses in our bodies can be triggered off by all sorts of things and not just by our thoughts. *Anchoring* is the word used to describe the link between a trigger or stimulus and a response. In other words, something in our environment – it could be a sound, a smell, a piece of music, a thought – triggers off a reaction in us. This reaction could be happiness, sadness, nervousness, anxiety, confidence, elation – responses that just happen automatically without your having much control over them, unless you become aware of what's happening.

Anchors are all around us: we can hear a specific piece of music and find ourselves filled with emotion. The music from a passing ice-cream van can trigger childhood memories.

Smells can produce particularly strong responses: the smell of a certain perfume can remind you of the excitement of a first date. But then again, the smell of a food that once gave you food poisoning can be enough to trigger a similarly bad response. These kinds of automatic responses are triggered inside us all through the day.

NLP anchoring is one of the most popular NLP techniques: It's easy to do and extremely powerful. It will give you the control to put yourself in the kind of states you like to be in, at the push of a button.

This link was originally discovered by Ivan Pavlov, the famous Russian scientist who carried out an experiment with his dogs. Each time the dogs were given some food, their mouths would begin to salivate in response. Pavlov decided to ring a bell each time he fed the dogs, so that pretty soon the dogs would begin to associate the ringing of the bell with food.

He then discovered that the sound of the bell was all that was needed to trigger off the salivation in the dogs, even if it wasn't feeding time and there was no food around for them to see or smell. Their bodies produced an automatic response (i.e. producing saliva) even if they were not hungry.

In NLP we use the same principles to create anchors, but this time we deliberately make links and form associations. Creating anchors in this way is a valuable skill that will enable you to change your feelings from an undesired state to a desired one:

- Self-doubt to confidence
- Procrastination to motivation
- Lethargy to boundless energy
- Stress to relaxation
- Anger to calm
- Melancholia to happiness
- Fear to courage.

Exercise: The Feelgood Anchor

This exercise requires you to close your eyes – you can either read through all the instructions before you begin so you understand all the steps, or you can invite a friend or colleague to read through the exercise for you.

You'll be asked to squeeze your thumb and middle finger together – for this exercise you'll need to be using those on your dominant hand, i.e. the hand that you write with.

1. Take a few moments to find somewhere comfortable to sit and make yourself relaxed.
2. Remind yourself of a time in the past when you felt really happy or good about yourself. Perhaps this was a time shared with friends or family, or a time at work when you were praised for doing something well.
3. Close your eyes and take yourself back to that time. See all that you saw, hear all that you heard and feel the feelings that you felt back then.
4. Become aware of what you're seeing in that picture, and make it a bit bigger. Turn the colours up brighter, bolder, stronger, and if there are any sounds in this memory of yours, turn the volume up louder.
5. Make that picture bigger and bring it closer to you.
6. If you can see yourself in that picture (i.e. you're dissociated), imagine floating up from your chair and sliding down into the *you* in that picture.
7. Become the *you* and really enjoy this moment once more.

8. Focus on this time in the past when you truly felt feelings of happiness.

9. As you continue to enjoy looking at this picture, become aware of where exactly in your body you're experiencing those feelings of happiness.

10. Locate those feelings and make them spin around even faster, allowing them to spread right through your body from the top of your head to the tips of your toes.

11. Keep running through these steps until you feel that wonderful feeling begin to peak.

12. As it becomes stronger and stronger, just squeeze the thumb and middle finger on your dominant hand together. Squeeze them tightly together, capturing all of those good, good feelings.

13. And release. Relax and open your eyes as you come back into the room.

14. Whenever you want to feel this good feeling again, all you're going to have to do is squeeze that thumb and middle finger together once more.

Running through this exercise several times a day will ensure that your 'feelgood anchor' becomes more powerful.

You can intensify the feelings attached to this anchor by remembering to squeeze that same thumb and middle finger together whenever anything good happens: a funny episode on TV or the radio, a good laugh with friends, praise or a compliment from someone close.

This NLP Anchoring Technique is featured here with the kind permission of Richard Bandler

Once you have established this anchor, you'll be able to summon up those same good feelings automatically, simply by squeezing that thumb and middle finger together once more. You can create more Anchors for yourself – check out apps 10, 15 and 18.

Live in the Moment

It's not uncommon for our minds to flip between the past (to things that happened even five minutes ago) and the future (to things you're planning). It's possible to completely 'miss the moment' in life and stumble through it without appreciating the good parts. How many of us rush through Christmas, for example, with only January's credit card bill as a reminder?

'Living in the moment', or 'mindfulness' as it's also known, is based on Buddhist philosophy and is a deliberate way of being. Research shows that people who practise the art of observation and deliberately make a point of noticing all the tiny details of each moment report decreased stress levels, a greater sense of happiness and are less likely to become ill. The benefits are certainly worth having and with just a little bit of practice you too can begin to live your life mindfully.

Aim to take a few moments each day to keep yourself in the present – notice what is going on around you and actively 'create memories' for yourself. Pretend you have a camera in your mind and take imaginary snapshots, noticing the good things as they happen – the smile on someone's face, good food, a sunny day, a feeling of wellbeing.

And as you notice each of these events, allow a feeling of gratitude to fill your body.

Case Study: The Dinner

Julie, a regular client of mine, came in to see me and complained about her husband 'never being able to enjoy anything'. She elaborated that she had suggested they go out to dinner and try a new restaurant that had recently opened up in town. She had heard good reports about it. However, whilst she'd had a great evening, her husband had moaned all the way through and failed to see what was so good about the place.

Despite the fact that they spent the time sitting at the same table and experiencing the same things, she felt as if they had experienced two separate evenings.

I asked a few questions about the evening and she told me what a lovely place it had been: the tables were nicely laid with starched linen tablecloths, flowers and candles; a live band provided the music; the waiters were friendly and the food was a delight.

Her husband, on the other hand, had been on edge all evening. He was worried about where he had parked the car, wondering if he had chosen the space unwisely – perhaps he'd end up with a ticket. They had left their children at home with a new babysitter and his mind seem to drift every now and then as he wondered how they were all getting along. He did not seem to notice the ambience of the restaurant and was even more unhappy when presented with the bill. He hoped his credit card could take the strain that month.

Julie felt very disappointed at the way things had gone. She had wanted them to spend some quality time together and yet they could have been at two completely different restaurants for all the good it had done.

I told Julie this was not an uncommon experience – it's not unusual to hear one person say they went to a terrific party and then hear another describe the same party as dreadful.

Julie was fully absorbed in the moment, taking in all the information through her senses – the sounds, the tastes, the smells, even the feel of the linen napkins. On the other hand, her husband had been completely dissociated, with his mind wandering to things going on outside. In all honesty, he might as well have stayed at home – for whilst his body may have been sitting in the restaurant with Julie, his mind certainly wasn't.

When it was pointed out to him, Julie's husband was able to recognise that his inability to live life 'in the moment' meant he was not getting as much pleasure out of simple experiences like a walk in the park or a meal in a restaurant as Julie. Fortunately, he was keen to change things and I showed him a few techniques to help.

> 'At every party there are two kinds of people – those who want to go home and those who don't. The trouble is, they are usually married to each other.'
>
> Ann Landers, American advice columnist

As our lives become busier and busier, it's not uncommon for people to lose the knack of 'living in the moment' – if this sounds like you, you can practise bringing yourself back into the moment by creating a running commentary for yourself in ~~the~~ your internal dialogue.

For example, next time you go for a walk outside, describe

everything that you see on your way: 'The leaves on that tree are very green; there's a brown dog running past; that lorry has big black wheels; the sun is shining brightly today; I can feel a warm breeze on my face; I can hear the sound of gravel as my feet stride across the path.'

You can also practise this on simple activities that you do around the house, such as washing your hands. 'I'm turning on the hot tap and now adding some cold water; the soap is green and cold to the touch; I'm squirting some on my left hand and now rubbing it against my right hand; it feels slippery; I am making rich white lather; now the water is gurgling down the plughole.'

To begin with this may feel rather strange, but remember, being able to associate more fully in your everyday life will heighten your experience of it. Practise this every day for a week and notice how your ability to see the fine details rapidly improves.

One final tip is to keep a notebook by the side of your bed and, at the end of each day, just before you go to sleep, write down three really positive things that happened that day. They can be as simple as 'it was a lovely sunny day today'. The important thing is to get your mind to automatically start seeking out the positive aspects of your life, rather than dwelling on the negative ones. It may be a bit of a chore to begin with but the benefits will be felt within a week or so and they are certainly worth having!

6

The Power of Belief

'Your beliefs become your thoughts
Your thoughts become your words
Your words become your actions
Your actions become your habits
Your habits become your values
Your values become your destiny'
Mahatma Gandhi

So far, we've had a look at how our senses absorb information from our environment and pass it on to our minds. Our minds then process this information and it becomes a thought.

We know that our thoughts are made up of pictures, language and feelings – which ultimately affect our behaviour and results. And we've discovered how easily we can alter these to suit our needs. But there is another area that has an effect on the outcome of our lives, and that is our beliefs.

'Whether you believe you can, or believe you can't – you're probably right.'

Henry Ford

One of my favourite stories that demonstrates the power of our beliefs is the story of Roger Bannister, the first person to run a mile in under four minutes, back in 1954. For many years, runners had dreamed of breaking the record but none had been successful. Indeed, doctors had declared it an impossibility, fearing the heart would spontaneously combust under the pressure. Bannister, however, was determined and against advice organised a race that saw him not only achieve his goal of four minutes, but beat it with seconds to spare. News of his achievement spread around the world.

Interestingly, while no one in the history of running had been able to achieve that record-breaking time, as soon as Bannister did it, other athletes went on to do the same over the course of the next year.

Are you surprised? Perhaps not very. But I'm sure you will be when I tell you how many broke the same record. Thirty-seven of them. Yes, thirty-seven in just one year!

It would not have been surprising if one or two more had achieved the same time, but the fact that so many runners went on to do it demonstrates that as soon as they had the concrete evidence that it really was possible, their performance automatically matched their altered beliefs.

The Placebo Effect

We're all familiar with the notion that our beliefs can both indirectly and directly affect our health. Medical research has proven that giving a patient a placebo can sometimes be as powerful as many drugs. But exactly why a fake, sugar-coated tablet should have such healing properties remains a bit of a mystery.

A startling example comes from an American study in the power of placebos in cancer patients. A group of cancer patients were given 'placebo chemotherapy' and, believing that it was the real thing, a third of them went on to lose all their hair. They went bald because they believed it was their fate.

And I wonder if you've ever fallen foul of the 'reverse placebo effect'? It can sometimes only take one person to announce that 'there's a bug going around' for everyone to start feeling a bit off colour.

Beliefs like that are working on us every day of our lives. They impinge on everything we do – our relationships, our health, our happiness, our success.

If we believe in positive things, life tends to go well; if we believe in negative things, we'll find ourselves falling flat on our faces.

Dr Bruce Lipton, the internationally recognised authority in bridging science and spirit, takes this all one step further. In his book *The Biology of Belief* he details new scientific discoveries that demonstrate the biochemical effects of the brain's functioning, showing that your thoughts actually affect all the cells in your body. As your beliefs control not only your behaviour but also your gene activity, they quite literally control your entire life.

Building beliefs is what human beings do. From a very young age we quickly accept and acquire the beliefs that are handed down to us from our parents, teachers and authority figures. We also acquire beliefs through our experiences – one bad trip to the dentist can lead you to believe that all dentists are bad and it's necessary to fear them all.

Unhelpful beliefs, such as this one, can hold us back, keeping us trapped in the same old habits of behaviour.

Put simply, your ability to change something in your life is going to be severely hampered if you do not believe that you will be able to do it.

Desperately wanting to lose weight, for example, is not going to be enough if you do not really believe that you'll ever get into those smaller jeans. Taking a driving test when you cannot really believe that you'll be able to drive around town independently is not a formula for success. No one ever visualised failure and found themselves being rewarded with success.

It's possible to increase your chances of success by literally changing your level of certainty about a potential outcome. In previous chapters you were able to practise changing the *submodalities* of the images your mind makes to enhance your wellbeing. It's possible to alter those images further by making them seem all the more believable and credible to you. For, as we know, if you believe something can happen, it's many, many times more likely to happen.

Exercise: Belief

1. Think of something that you have a strong sense of certainty about – for example, what you had for lunch yesterday.
2. Notice where the picture appears and make a note of the submodalities – the fine details about that picture – location, size, colour, sounds, frame, etc. Take a few moments to do this – there's no rush.
3. Now I want to stand up and shake your body around, to clear your mind.
4. Then sit down once more and this time think of something that you're uncertain about – for example, what you think you might be having for lunch tomorrow.
5. Again, notice where the picture appears and make a note of those fine details – its location, size, colour, moving or still etc.

You will most probably have discovered that your 'strong certainty' pictures appear in a different place to those that you're uncertain about.

Test this out further by coming up with more examples, such as: How you celebrated your last birthday / how you expect to be celebrating your next one. Where you went on holiday last year / where you might go in two or three years' time. The make of car you drive / what car you might buy next time.

Now complete this submodality check to establish the difference between the two answers you came up with in each case.

Visual Submodalities	**Certainty**	**Uncertainty**
Location		
Colour/black and white		
Associated or dissociated		
Size		
Brightness		
Still or moving		
Shape		
Framed or panoramic		
Focused or fuzzy		

Auditory Submodalities	**Certainty**	**Uncertainty**
Volume		
Pitch		
Tonality		
Rhythm		
Direction of voice		
Duration		

Kinaesthetic Submodalities	**Certainty**	**Uncertainty**
Location in body		
Temperature		
Shape		
Pressure		
Size		
Breathing rate		
Direction of movement		

Exercise: Certainty

1. Think of something you'd like to achieve, but about which you've been doubting your chances of success.
2. Look carefully at the picture your mind creates for you and imagine gently picking it up in your hand and placing it in the position where you saw all those pictures of strong belief or certainty.
3. Once it's in place, check that the submodalities – all those fine details – match those good pictures.
4. Do whatever you need to do it get it looking just right – stretch it, add colour, a frame, make it a still or movie, add voices – whatever you know you need to make it become a strong belief.

Look at this picture in this position several times a day and notice how your feelings gradually change – as your original negative feelings become positive you'll develop a feeling of absolute certainty about succeeding.

Now that you have your 'belief formula', you'll be able to start recognising the differences between your strong beliefs and those you are less certain about.

Next time you find yourself wondering if it's ever going to be possible for you to achieve that goal of yours – be it to lose weight, quit smoking, apply for a new job or stand up and give a speech – creating an image in your mind with the same submodalities as those in your 'Certainty' column is going to massively increase your chances of success.

The Danish physicist Niels Bohr, when asked whether he really believed a horseshoe hanging over his door would bring him luck, answered: 'Of course not, but I am told it works even if you don't believe in it.'

7

Goal!

So now you're equipped with more knowledge about the way your mind works than you've perhaps ever had before. But is this going to be enough to enable you to set about fixing those irritating problems that just hold you back in life?

Well, it may well be – but then again, how many times in the past have you known exactly *what* to do, but putting it into practice just wasn't that easy and you quickly found yourself giving up?

That's because *how* you approach your problems can also mean the difference between success and failure. We all know what we need to do to lose weight, for example – eat less and move more – but putting it into practice isn't always that easy. Getting yourself a 'success plan' in place before you start tinkering around with those NLP apps is going to be just as important.

Designing a New Life

We all know people who just seem to 'get it right', but precisely why is it that some of us are more successful than others?

Whether you have a specific problem you'd like to tackle, such as losing weight, or you'd like your entire life to take on a new direction, having a clear plan of how you are going to do this will make all the difference.

Whether you're seeking to fix a small problem or have a complete overhaul of your life, it's good to begin by taking stock. It can be easy to focus on what isn't working for us, but it's equally important to become aware of what is and does work very well, for this is the beginning of creating that 'success strategy' for yourself.

Compare your life now to this time last year. What changes did you create and how many changes 'happened' or were thrust upon you? And what's stayed the same? If you had a chance to replay that year over again, what would you do differently? And how are things working for you at the moment?

The Wheel of Life

It's very easy to come up with a list of all the things we'd like to change in our lives – perhaps you've done this many times before. And like most people, you probably went on to discover that you actually ended up fixing very few of those problems. The list became overwhelming as you spread yourself far too thinly to achieve anything meaningful. The lack of success then knocked back your confidence and motivation and it became easier to abandon the hope of ever changing anything. Knowing where to begin and beginning in the right place is the key to making things work for you in the future.

Step 1: Take stock of your life right now by completing the following chart. You'll see various categories for all the areas of your life. Ask yourself how well things are going in each of these categories. Take a pen and give yourself a score out of 10, then shade in the segment accordingly. The closer you get to the centre of the circle, the closer you are to scoring full marks, and if you are really dissatisfied give yourself a lower score and shade in less, keeping yourself nearer the edge of the circle.

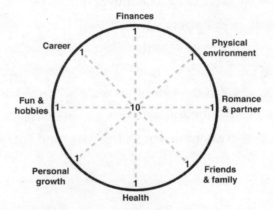

Step 2: When you have completed your chart, think about each of the categories, one at a time, and ask yourself this – if everything in this area of my life was simply brilliant and deserved being given a score of 10, how many of the other categories would benefit as a result? Give each category a second score in this way.

The category that gets the highest ranking on the second scores is where you should aim to start fixing things first, for the impact on the rest of your life will be the greatest. And the quicker you can begin to experience results, the more motivated you'll be to fix all the other areas.

Goal-setting for Success

Most of us are used to setting goals and targets for ourselves in the form of New Year's resolutions. Think back to some of the ones you've set for yourself in the past and become aware of your successes, and then also your failures.

Like most people, you can probably count the successes on the fingers of one hand, whilst being able to make a long, long list of all those you failed to achieve. Often made on the spur of the moment or fuelled by alcohol, it's not surprising that most of us have forgotten about them by the second week of January.

In NLP we prefer to use the word 'outcome' rather than target or goal. It's not difficult to set a goal – 'I want to lose weight' or 'I want to earn more money', but having a clearly defined outcome for yourself is what's going to make the difference. In other words, a 'goal' is something we want, whilst an 'outcome' is the result we get. As the results we get are not always what we'd like, for clarity NLP suggests that you refer to them as your 'desired outcomes'.

But even then it's possible for your desired outcomes to be fuzzy and not completely thought-through – they can be ill-formed with unforeseen pitfalls waiting to trip you up.

NLP has a model that when followed enables you to clearly define and structure your goal with 'well-formed conditions' for your outcome. I suggest that you follow this structure for every result you want to achieve, whether it be an irritating little habit that you want to rid yourself of, or a major life-changing ambition you'd like to realise.

Setting your outcome involves taking time to consider your goal and what you will gain, and, having done this, you'll be able to direct your focus or your 'success spotlight' in the right way at the right time, making you more likely to succeed.

The Well-formed Outcomes Model

Answer each of these questions to clarify your goal. Write down your answers and use them to create a clear and precise success plan:

1. **Is the goal stated in positive terms?** 'I want to be slimmer and fitter' rather than 'I don't want to be fat any longer'. 'I want to feel calm and relaxed about the future' rather than 'I want to stop worrying'. 'I want to start earning more money' rather than 'I want to stop struggling financially'.

2. **Can you achieve this goal by yourself, without being dependent on anyone else for assistance?** If your desired outcome depends on someone else's actions, then it is not considered to be an acceptable outcome. 'I want to earn more money' is acceptable if you're self-employed or in a sales environment that means your income is governed by your personal efforts, but is it an acceptable outcome if you're a public-sector worker who's waiting for the government to announce the next round of pay rises? Perhaps you need to be aiming for a promotion, or thinking about other ways you could earn extra money.

3. **Is the context clearly defined? How will it be achieved – when, where, how, who?** Having established your goal, be very specific about what it is you're aiming for. If you want to lose weight – exactly how much do you want to lose and by when? Is there a specific reason for losing weight (e.g. I want to be a size 12 in time for my summer holiday in July)?

   A larger outcome – such as wanting that promotion – may have to be broken into smaller chunks. Will you need to do some more studying, pass an exam, acquire new skills or gain more experience?

4. **Have you included all your senses when stating your goal? What will you see, feel and hear when you have achieved it? And what about other people – what will they see, feel and hear when you have achieved it?** Following on from the previous point, once you have defined your outcome in specific terms, you'll need to establish some sensory-based evidence. How will you know when you have reached your goal? You can close your eyes here and imagine yourself at a time in the future when you have achieved all that you want to achieve. And what will other people around you be saying? If you're chasing that promotion, for example, what kind of things will your staff be saying? What other things around you will let you know that you have achieved your goal? Will you be eating in more expensive restaurants or holidaying in more exotic locations?

5. **Does the outcome fit in with your life and personal values? Is it meaningful for you?** Think carefully about how your goal will impact others around you. Would you really want that promotion if it meant travelling away from home for weeks at a time and being separated from your loved ones? Or is spending time at home with the family more important to you? Asking yourself questions like 'When don't I want this outcome?' will enable you set appropriate boundaries for yourself.

6. **Will achieving this goal still preserve those aspects of your life you'd like to retain?** Think carefully about whether you stand to lose anything in your life as a result of achieving this goal. All of our bad habits and behaviour have some sort of positive pay-offs, otherwise we wouldn't do them. Smoking cigarettes and drinking alcohol, for example, help people to relax. It's important to take into account the positive benefits of these negative behaviours or they'll self-sabotage your attempts. Now, it may be that giving up smoking or drinking will make you feel much more relaxed anyway because you no longer have to worry about your health or the money you would normally be spending. But you may have to find other ways to help you feel relaxed such as taking more exercise. Think about these things before you begin making changes.

7. **Have you identified the resources you'll need?** What will you need to get you started and what will you need further down the line? Have you ever done this before? Would

you benefit from getting advice from someone who has done this before? Is there more than one way to achieve this outcome? Which way will be best for you?

8. **What's your first step going to be? And then the next?**
Having ensured that your outcome is now 'well-formed', you'll need to clearly define that first step into action. What will it be? If your goal or target feels enormous and almost out of reach, break it down into smaller ones. Your first step needs to be manageable because if you do not take it, you will not take any of the others either. Perhaps your first step will be picking up the telephone and asking someone for advice. What will the next steps be?

Once you have answered each of these questions and feel you have a good idea of what you're going to be working towards, you can write your success plan using the **S.M.A.R.T.** acronym. This is commonly used in business and stands for:

S   Specific
M   Measurable
A   Achievable
R   Realistic
T   Time-bound

Here are two examples of a success plan:

'It is 21 July and I weigh 65 kg. I am exercising every day by walking the dog and attend yoga classes twice a week. I am wearing

size 10 jeans and feel fitter than I have done in years. My family appreciate my new-found energy and give me many compliments.'

'It is 3 January and I have started my new job. Having studied hard and gained those extra qualifications, I can now command a higher salary of £XXX. I have paid off my credit card debts and have been able to buy a new car.'

In each of these examples, a time frame was set for those goals – if you don't set a time, you're less likely to achieve your desired outcome. You'll notice that the success was specific and measurable: the size 10 jeans and the higher salary. After all, you need to know when you've reached your target.

And the goals set were realistic, which is perhaps the most important part of being successful. Give yourself completely unrealistic goals such as 'I want to be a billionaire by this time next week' and you're setting yourself up for failure.

Make your goal realistic and, once you've reached it, you can always set another one that will take you a few steps further on. Set the bar too high and you'll set yourself up for failure. Set it too low and you'll feel that you're not very capable.

Carrot or Stick

People either invest time, energy and resources moving 'towards' a particular goal or 'away from' something they'd rather avoid. Working out which category you fall into can assist you in creating a well-formed outcome that suits your personality.

In the previous exercises, did you find yourself wanting *more* of things or *less* of things?

And what about in your day-to-day life? When you walk into a crowded room at a party, do you automatically start looking for those people you would like to speak to *or* do you quickly scan the room for those you want to avoid?

When you choose where to go on holiday, do you base your choice on what you *do* want – nice beach, good hotel, interesting sights – or do you base your choice on what you *don't* want – long journey, dodgy food, mosquitoes?

What motivates you to work hard? Is it the prospect of a promotion, more money and a bigger house? Or is the fear that if you don't work hard, you might lose your job, your home and even your family?

Think back to when you purchased your last car: did you make your decision based on safety and economy or performance and design?

If you want to lose weight, what picture motivates you more: seeing yourself in a slim pair of jeans, or the thought and fear of going up a few dress sizes if you don't take action now?

All of this information will help you to tailor and design your goals in such a way as to fit in with your motivational style. Neither pattern is better than the other, but it is useful to be aware of the benefits and also the pitfalls of each.

People who put a lot of energy into moving 'towards' their goals can sometimes get so excited about their future that they don't pay sufficient attention to the possible pitfalls. A lack of instant success can then bring about a lack of motivation.

Exercise: Towards or Away?

1. Advertisers often use this powerful pattern when they set out to sell to you. Have a look through the advertisements in magazines and see if you can spot this 'away from' or 'towards' kind of language.
2. Identifying this driving pattern in other people can help you to gain more influence or persuasion over them as you tailor your presentation or argument to answer the questions in their minds – before they've even asked them.

Those people who get used to using an 'away from' pattern can sometimes get side-tracked by the many potential problems they're trying to dodge. Over-cautiousness can sometimes prevent them from moving forward.

Measuring Success

Think back to those New Year's resolutions of yours: what were you aiming for this time last year?

Like most people, you've probably completely forgotten! And that is one of the reasons why you failed to reach your target. Out of sight, out of mind, as they say.

America's top success coach, Michael Neill, is fond of telling people that if every morning they stopped to tell a lamp-post what their goals were for the day, they would stand a better chance of succeeding than if they kept them to themselves. As strange as this may seem, it's good advice!

Now whilst I'm not advocating that you wander out into the street and start babbling away to inanimate objects, it's clear that if you express your thoughts and ideas, making them more tangible, you'll know exactly in which direction you need to point yourself. You'll also be able to measure your success and reposition yourself if things are not going according to plan. Otherwise, how will you know?

Diary of Proof: Keeping track of your progress will spur you on to even greater success. From now on it's going to be important to behave a little like a detective, collecting evidence and proof that you're moving closer to your goal each day.

Studies have shown that 'what gets measured, improves', so start noticing the small changes that are taking place in your life and record them each day in a small notebook.

And do remember that it's the direction in which you're going, rather than the speed at which you're travelling, that's the most important thing.

Celebrate how close you are to getting what you desire, remembering to always focus on what you do want rather than on what you don't. This will mean the difference between success and failure for you.

8

Get in the Right State

It's important to remember that the techniques that I'm going to introduce you to in this book are the sort of techniques that an NLP practitioner would use in a session with a client.

As you're not in a face-to-face session with me, but learning how to take control of your own mind through a book, I'm going to suggest that you get yourself 'in the right state' each time before you carry out the visualisation exercises for yourself.

The average session with me lasts around an hour and a half and I can spend around forty minutes of that time unravelling the problem and getting my client ready to make changes. By my using hypnotic language conversationally, my clients relax and begin to feel positive about their new future.

We are all able to visualise, but some people find it a little more difficult to relax, drift off and dream than others. Often they can be quick to dismiss the techniques, feeling that somehow they are just not working. So, before you attempt to work on yourself, take some time to relax by using the following exercises:

Exercise: Basic Breathing

1. With your hand on the area above your navel, tighten up your stomach muscles so that they tuck in. Hold the tension for a moment.
2. Now let the muscles relax and feel the difference.
3. Repeat steps 1 and 2. You are now beginning to become aware of what the difference between tension and relaxation in that area feels like.
4. Now breathe in through the nose in such a way that your hand is pushed up by the inflated stomach region. Hold your breath for a moment.
5. Now breathe out through the mouth and notice how your stomach deflates and how this makes your hand go down again.
6. Repeat steps 4 and 5 twenty times and notice how you become progressively calmer as you are doing this exercise.

Exercise: Counting Breath

1. Close your eyes.
2. Breathe in so your stomach area rises up, then breathe out and, in your mind, count '1'. Keep your attention on your breathing only, don't let other thoughts intrude.
3. Continue breathing in and out, and each time you breathe out, count the next number in your mind. Concentrate on your breathing only.

What number did you get to before you found your mind wandering off? To make it easier to get into the higher figures there are a couple of things you can do to help:

a) When you say a number in your mind, create a picture of it too.

b) Focus intently on the various sensations and movements that happen in the trunk of your body while you are breathing in and out.

As your body relaxes, your mind will also begin to feel restful.

Exercise: Muscle Relaxation

Hands:	Clench each fist (one at a time) for three seconds and then relax each hand for three seconds.
Arms:	Bend each elbow so the wrist nearly touches the shoulder (one at a time) and hold for three seconds, then relax each arm for a further three seconds.
Legs:	Point the toes and straighten the leg, pushing the knee down, so both the calf and thigh muscles tighten for three seconds, then relax this leg for three seconds. Repeat with the other leg.
Bottom:	Squeeze the bottom as if trying to lift it off the bed or chair for three seconds, then relax it for three seconds.
Stomach:	Pull the stomach in and hold for three seconds, then relax it for three seconds.
Chest:	Stick the chest out like a bodybuilder and take a deep breath in, hold it for three seconds, then relax for a further three seconds.

Shoulders and neck:	Pull the shoulders up to the ears (or as close as they can get), and hold for three seconds, then relax for a further three seconds.
Mouth:	Clench the teeth and make a big, wide smile and hold for three seconds, then relax the mouth completely for three seconds.
Eyes:	Scrunch up the eyes so that they are tightly shut for three seconds, then relax the eyes, but keep them shut for at least three seconds.
Forehead:	Put a hand on the head to make sure it does not move. Raise the eyes to look at the ceiling so that the forehead becomes wrinkled. Hold for three seconds and relax for three seconds.

Self-hypnosis

Avoid self-hypnosis if you have a history of epilepsy. Never attempt to induce a trance-like state when driving or operating machinery.

Allowing yourself to drift into an even deeper trance-like state can be very useful for visualising solutions to problems and setting goals. Find a place to practise where you'll be free from distractions and disturbances.

The Eye-fixation Technique:
1. Make yourself comfortable and sit in a quiet place. Take a few deep breaths and stare straight in front of you.

2. Find a spot on the wall or ceiling ahead of you and begin staring at it.

3. Continue to focus all your attention on this spot. Keep your gaze fixed on it at all times, avoiding blinking. People often report that the spot becomes fuzzy or distorted.

4. After a few moments (it varies from person to person), you'll find your eyelids beginning to feel heavy as you continue to stare.

5. Keep your breathing deep and even. When you feel as if you no longer want to keep your eyes open – because your eyelids feel too heavy or your eyes begin to smart, gently close them.

6. As you close your eyes, enjoy the feeling of relaxation that you get from doing so.

7. Your breathing can begin to slow right down as you become aware of a wave of relaxation spreading through your body from the top of your head, all the way through to the tip of your toes.

8. Now you are comfortably relaxed, you can spend some time working towards your goals of positive change.

9. When you are ready, you can open your eyes – suggest to yourself that when you do you will feel refreshed and alert.

Thought Field Therapy

Dr Roger Callahan, an eminent American psychologist, developed Thought Field Therapy (TFT) some twenty-three years ago, to help rid people of all sorts of negative emotions. He discovered that tapping a specific sequence of acupuncture points in the body, whilst at the same time thinking about the problem, will quickly reduce your levels of anxiety or stress.

The process may seem a bit strange at first but independent scientific research has shown that it works. Levels of cortisol (our stress hormone) reduce significantly after using the tapping technique and heart rate variability improves, contributing to our wellbeing.

When I first started using the technique with clients in 2004, I was often asked if I had hidden cameras in the room – so convinced were people that this was some kind of wind-up.

Just recently, however, a lady came to see me having actually been advised by her GP to learn the technique, as he felt she would benefit from it. This rapid shift in perception, from something slightly alternative to a technique that even the NHS are beginning to sit up and take note of, is partly due to Paul McKenna. Over the past five years, Paul has been bringing TFT to a larger audience through his television appearances and by including it in his books. Initially even he was surprised to find himself so taken with the meridian therapy, but his desire to help people feel better soon outweighed any scepticism.

It's a technique that I now use with all my clients and it's especially effective for overcoming feelings of negativity. As with all the techniques I'm mentioning, it's best to read through the instructions carefully before you try them out for yourself.

TFT for Relaxation: There are a number of points that you will be required to tap around your body and it's best to stick to the sequence of points as detailed here. You can use two fingers to do the tapping – your index and middle fingers.

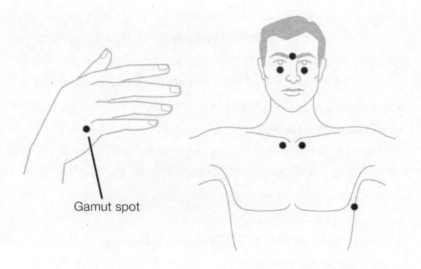

Gamut spot

1. Tap five times between your eyebrows with one of your hands.

2. Tap five times under your eye just on the cheekbone (doesn't matter which one).

3. Tap five times under your arm (a couple of inches below the armpit).

4. Use both hands and tap five times just under your collar-
   bone (in the middle of your chest).

5. Locate gamut spot (see diagram). Whilst you are tapping
   this point at the side of your hand:

   • Close your eyes.

   • Open your eyes and look down to the left.

   • Now look down to the right.

   • Circle your eyes 360 degrees around in one direction.

   • Circle your eyes around in the opposite direction.

   • Hum a few bars of any tune out loud.

   • Count out loud from one to five.

   • Hum the tune again.

Relax your hands and notice how your body is beginning to
relax. Now take a nice deep breath and repeat points 1–4 once
more. At the end of this tapping sequence, you'll be feeling
more relaxed than before and ready to begin your visualisation exercises.

9

Fix Your Habits and Motivation

'Bad habits are like chains that are too light to feel ... until they are too heavy to carry.'
Warren Buffett, billionaire investor and business guru

Like most people, you've probably set yourself goals and targets in the past, only to quickly discover that that was the easy part. Summoning up the strength, energy and commitment to see things through to a conclusion can prove more challenging.

So, in this section, I'll be showing you how easy it can be to get pumped up and motivated in order to make those habit changes. They say that preparation is 90 per cent of success and when it comes to achieving goals, getting yourself in the right *state* or frame of mind can mean the difference between success and failure.

Over the years, you've programmed your mind with many different patterns of behaviour. These patterns get stored as habits and they enable you to operate on 'automatic pilot' – for example, you no longer have to think about *how* to tie your shoelaces, you can do it without thinking – you've developed your own shortcuts.

Having the ability to create your own 'autopilot' can be really handy, but what happens when you've acquired a bad habit and decide you want to 'unlearn' that piece of behaviour and make changes? Most people find that their subconscious minds are so efficient at hanging on to habits that it can become a real struggle to make changes. It's not surprising that willpower alone often fails to make a difference. In order to successfully change a habit you'll need to change the 'programming' too.

Over time, our habits become enmeshed with each other and form a kind of 'network' in our minds – they connect with each other. You just know that if you eat a chocolate bar on the way home from work for a few days running, you'll then miss it if you cut it out and your journey home will start to feel uncomfortable.

Changing one small thing in our lives can sometimes seem difficult, so making a few other *minor* changes at the same time can help to release that stranglehold, for a change of routine is enough to confuse the 'habit' part of our mind.

You can start seizing back control of your life by simply taking a few small steps. For example:

1. **Travel:** Choose a different route to get yourself to work.

2. **Newspaper/magazine:** Read a different one.

3. **Radio:** Change station or start listening to the radio again.

4. **Food:** Be adventurous and try something you've never eaten before.

5. **Toiletries:** Change your regular brand of shampoo and shower gel.

6. **Sport/exercise:** Try something new like yoga, tai chi or table tennis.

7. **Watch a live sports event:** Choose any event and go and watch it.

8. **TV:** Watch something you wouldn't normally consider.

9. **Contact:** Get in touch with a long-lost friend or relation.

10. **Shift:** Sit in a different place from your usual one and even move the furniture around.

11. **Charity work:** Choose any local group and go and help out.

12. **Cinema:** Go by yourself to watch a film.

Waiting for the Right Time

'I just need to be in the right frame of mind' is a sentence that most of us have uttered at some time or another. Getting on and doing something, whether it's losing weight, quitting smoking, filling out a tax return or clearing out a cupboard is always that much easier to do 'in the right frame of mind'.

But as most of us have discovered, sitting around waiting for that magical moment could just mean never getting started at all. How many things in your life just keep getting put to the bottom of your 'to-do' list, and how many more will there be over the next few years?

Not only are you not getting started – you're also making it harder to ever start at all as your body will simply get into the habit of putting it off. The more we put off doing something, the less likely we are to ever start at all.

Wouldn't it be good if you could change the way you approach a situation instead of feeling powerless and stuck in a rut? One way to increase your options is to become aware of how you 'code' those experiences by becoming aware of the *submodalities*. These fine distinctions in your memories can make the difference between being in a positive, motivated state and one in which getting started will be an uphill struggle.

Psychological research has shown that people are most likely to make changes in their lives as a result of two things happening.

The first is a big life change occurring that may be beyond our control – a relationship breakdown, a change of job or moving house, for example. With so much getting tipped up into the air, those niggly day-to-day habits that once seemed so hard to break just lose their grip as we set about creating a new pattern of 'normal' for ourselves.

The other moment at which we are most likely to change is when we have quite simply 'had enough'. Whether it's an embarrassing moment in a communal changing room, an illness or injury, a comment from a friend or family member, we all have that 'tipping point' when enough is quite simply enough.

Rather than sitting around hoping that one day we'll get to that point, NLP can help you speed up the process and enable you to flick that switch to get up and changing, right here, right now.

Follow these steps and get your life on the move:

1. Take a few moments to think about five times when your bad habit made you feel embarrassed, exhausted, depressed, angry or tearful. Write these episodes down on a piece of paper and take at least fifteen minutes to do this.

2. Now, make a movie in your mind of the first example you came up with. Have yourself see everything clearly – make it a big picture, turning the colours up brighter and stronger, and make sure you turn the volume up on any sounds in this image too. Run this moment through from start to finish.

3. Repeat this for the second memory, and then the third and the fourth and the fifth.

4. Take these five mini-movies and put them together, one after the other, so they link up as one continuous

movie of you looking unhappy and drained by this habit.

5. Run this movie through in your mind and have a good look at it – see your humiliation in glorious Technicolor. And then run it from start to finish again.

6. As you watch this horror movie unfolding, remember to make it really colourful and large.

7. Keep doing this to the point where you starting saying to yourself, 'I've had enough of this . . . I've had enough of this . . . I've had enough of this.' And keep repeating this.

This technique will push you over the edge, through that threshold, and crank up your desire to change. After all, why would you want to wait any longer when you've so much to gain from starting right now?

What's My Reward?

My clients often ask me if it's a good idea to introduce rewards as an additional incentive to changing habits. On the face of it, it does sound like a good idea – human beings are naturally goal-seeking individuals and surely if you're going to have to push yourself in order to achieve something, then rewarding yourself with an additional carrot may well make all the difference.

Many of us have in the past promised ourselves a weekend trip away, for example, in return for losing weight or passing exams. In fact, contrary to popular belief, our interest in completing a task – our intrinsic motivation – begins to rapidly *decline* if we introduce an extrinsic reward.

As soon as you take your attention, your awareness and focus away from your goal, you begin to make it much harder for yourself to succeed. You're going to need to direct every ounce of vital brainpower into focusing on the task in hand and how you're going to succeed.

A well-known experiment carried out in 1975 by the psychologist Edward L. Deci and colleagues featured two groups of students who were invited to work on an interesting puzzle. One half of the group was paid to do this and for the other half there was no reward involved.

It was discovered that the group who received no payment ended up being significantly more keen to continue to play with the puzzle in their free time. It was also reported that they showed more enthusiasm for the task and were able to engage with it more and as a result were more successful. The other group's eye was clearly looking in the direction of the financial reward and as a result they did all that was asked of them and no more.

Many experiments have been carried out since, with variations in the task assigned and the reward offered. In each case, the results have been replicated, with the conclusion that more pleasure and success can be derived from a task if there's no distracting element such as a reward.

Of course, there has to be something positive to be gained out of any kind of task, otherwise there would be no point in doing it. But keeping your end goal in sight as your 'reward' is going to increase your chances of getting there.

So, quitting smoking in order to be healthier and have more money in your pocket is better than doing it because someone has offered you a holiday as a reward. Losing weight in order to look more attractive and feel more energetic is more likely to spur you on and enable you to keep the weight off than the offer of a new car if you reach your target.

Delayed Gratification: For most people, delaying gratification is manageable provided the goal is quite short term – filing paperwork, for example. When the goal is a longer-term one such as studying for exams or a weight loss that may take many months, delaying gratification can seem that much harder.

Fortunately, it's possible to start experiencing right now all the good feelings you'll be feeling when you have achieved your goal. By taking a look into your future you'll be able to flood your body with those feelgood chemicals and allow them to propel you towards the future you desire so much. Remember, physiologically speaking our bodies can't distinguish between a real and an imagined event – we've all experienced this when reading thriller or horror stories. As your eyes track across the words on the page, your body synchronises and can make your heart beat a little bit faster and your hands feel sweaty.

In just the same way, it's possible to vividly imagine your wonderful new future and get all the benefits of feeling great right now.

Exercise: It's a Wonderful Life

As with all these techniques, read through this exercise carefully to begin with and then find a quiet place where you can relax and allow your imagination to take over. You can work with a friend and have them read the instructions slowly out loud, if you prefer.

1. Close your eyes, relax and imagine that you're walking into a cinema. Walk into the auditorium and take a seat near the front.

2. As you look up at the screen, you see that the film showing is in fact your very own *success movie*. A film of you in the future, having reached your target and achieved those goals – whatever it is you have in mind to achieve.

3. Take a good look at that movie now as you can see yourself doing all the things you wanted to be doing and accomplishing them with ease.

4. Add a splash of colour to this movie and turn the brightness up, making everything bolder and brighter.

5. Turn the volume up and listen carefully as you hear the sounds of success.

6. Notice those good feelings begin to travel around your body.

7. Take a good look at yourself: how you talk; how you walk; what kind of clothes you wear; the tone of your voice; what kind of places you go to; what kind of people you are mixing with.

8. See what you see, hear what you hear and feel how good this moment feels.

9. Keep making adjustments to this success movie of yours until it looks just the way you'd like it to look.

10. When things look pretty good, imagine yourself floating up out of that cinema seat and up into the screen in front of you. Become the 'you' in this success movie.

11. Now run that movie through again from start to finish with you in the starring role. Think through what it's like to see things from this angle and what it might help you to achieve. How much better does this feel now?

Spend as long as you like experiencing this new future of yours and, when you've finished, you can open your eyes and come back into the present moment.

Remember, if at any time in the future you feel yourself starting to flag or get weary with pursuing your goals, all you're going to have to do is transport yourself into this movie and remind yourself of why you are doing this. You'll be able to get a feel for the benefits in advance and it will help you more in the long run than any other kind of compensatory gift, treat or reward.

Keeping a Check on those Pictures

As we've already discovered, our minds are constantly making pictures as we think and speak. Take a few moments now to think about where you make your most helpful and unhelpful pictures when trying to motivate yourself.

1. Think about something that you just haven't been able to summon up the motivation for – exercising, eating less, weeding the garden, the pile of ironing: something that really doesn't seem all that appealing right now.

Let that picture grow in your mind and become aware of its location – perhaps it's a little to the left of your field of vision, maybe a little to the right. Perhaps it's high up or a bit lower down. Don't worry too much about the details but continue to think about the task that you're really not motivated to do.

2. Now erase that picture and think about something that you'd be really motivated to do – meet a particular friend for lunch, go to the pub, watch a football game, have a spa day.

Notice the picture. Have a really good look at it and notice the direction in which you feel your eyes moving. This is your 'good place' for making pictures. Now move picture 1 into the place where you noticed picture 2. Imagine picking up that pile of ironing, that tax return – whatever it was – and put in the place where the football match or lunch date appeared.

Just allow it to sit in this place and notice how your feelings towards that task gradually change. And perhaps you can allow that picture to develop slightly: allowing yourself to seeing a completed tax return rather than a blank, unstarted one.

Each time you think about tackling this task in the future, make sure you have that picture of whatever it is in your 'good place'.

Chunking Up and Chunking Down

We naturally organise information into chunks without realising it – think about how long telephone numbers get organised into smaller groups of numbers, for example. Some of us prefer to see the bigger picture whilst others prefer to pay attention to the small details. Getting to know your personal preference and 'chunking style' will enable you to keep yourself motivated once you've decided to fix a particular problem.

If the task in front of you seems daunting, try chunking it down into smaller, more manageable parts. For example, if you're attempting to lose weight, setting your target at two pounds per week may be of greater use to you than one of three stones in total.

And when you feel there are just too many details for you to cope with – you can't see the wood for the trees – then chunking up will help you to see the overall purpose or meaning of your goal. This strategy is particularly helpful if you're working with a team or group of people with conflicting opinions. Directing everyone's attention to the bigger picture can diffuse disagreements as it becomes clearer that everyone is working towards the same goal.

Time to Take Your Temperature

As you think about your goal, have a look at the scale below and take a reading. How high is your motivation at the moment? 10 is very high, pumped up and motivated, and zero means just that – a big, fat zero.

10 9 8 7 6 5 4 3 2 1 0

If you find yourself needing a bit more motivation to get yourself off that sofa, go to your apps and download app 15.

Top Tips for Getting Things Moving

1. Recognise excuses for what they are. If some mundane task (like doing the ironing) keeps getting in between you and your goal, ask yourself, 'What's the worst thing that can

happen if I do not do the ironing right now?' and 'What's the best thing that will happen?'

2. Ask yourself those same questions with regards to your goal – 'What's the worst thing that can happen if I do not aim for this goal?' and 'What's the best thing that can happen if I *do* aim for this goal?'

3. Fear of the unknown often holds us back – if you're not sure how things will turn out then do some research, get information, find out the facts and then decide what to do.

4. Beware of your internal dialogue – have you been silently criticising yourself or predicting a failed outcome before you've even started? Mind your language.

5. Chunk your goal down into smaller steps and see if this helps to get you started.

6. Limit your list-making to a maximum of four steps only. As you complete the first couple of steps, delete them and add new ones.

7. Or, if you can't seem to get started, why not start in the middle if a project seems overwhelming? Skip out the beginning bit and return to it later.

8. Keep reminding yourself what is important to you about achieving this goal. Write it down.

Case Study: Start Exercising

David had reached his fortieth birthday weighing eighteen stone. He had always been on the large side and a combination of factors meant that he had continued to gradually put on weight throughout his life. The milestone birthday had not been the time of celebration it should have been and a year later David had a medical at work that spelt out the facts – he needed to do something about his weight once and for all.

He followed a conventional diet, successfully losing three stones, but had recently plateaued. He seemed to need to eat less and less food to achieve any kind of weight loss and was by now seriously starting to lose motivation. Exercise had never been one of his strong points and in fact he hated it – at school he'd been the laughing stock as his feeble attempts on the football pitch were ridiculed. He knew that in order to lose more weight, he'd have to start doing some form of exercise but as he felt so tired all the time he just didn't have the energy.

Our childhood imprints: Our behaviour patterns result from our experiences and the beliefs we've picked up and developed, from our childhoods through to the present day. They become almost tattooed on our minds and create our self-image.

David had been teased at school for his clumsy efforts during PE lessons and on the sports field. Any efforts to take exercise as an adult had usually ended miserably – his large size made sporting activities difficult and, all around him, his friends seemed much more fit and able than he was. No wonder he avoided exercise like the plague. The years had taken their toll and David had ended up with a set of negative beliefs about his ability to take exercise and had even started to doubt that there were any positive benefits to doing so.

Step 1 – Changing Beliefs: Because it's very much harder to make changes if you just don't *believe* that this is something that you could be capable of doing, I started work here.

David described himself as someone who never took any exercise – a complete couch potato. I asked him what he meant by 'exercise' and he told me that he never went to the gym, joined his friends on the golf course, took skiing holidays or cycled anywhere. His motivation to do anything like this was completely at zero. Why would he want to do things that would only make him feel stupid?

He realised, of course, that now things would have to change but couldn't work out how he could get started.

I asked him if it would help if we changed the word 'exercise' and used 'activity' instead. I asked him if he could come up with a few examples of times where he is, or has been, active in his life. He came up with the following:

- Walks to shops at lunchtime to buy sandwich – thirty minutes.
- Walked neighbour's dog when they went on holiday – twice a day.
- Mows his mother's lawn every other week.
- Pruned trees and shrubs in the winter.
- Delivered leaflets to local area as part of work promotion.

Already we were starting to build up a picture of David as being someone who doesn't mind activity – when there is a purpose or reason attached to it, he doesn't give it a second thought. In fact, being useful in this way made him feel good about himself.

We brainstormed for a few minutes as I asked to him think if there was any other area in his life where he could help people out. He came up with a local council scheme to clear out the ponds on the nearby common. They were looking for volunteers who could give up the next few weekends.

If only he could get himself up off the sofa. Every time he thought about this extra activity, he quickly saw a picture of his sofa, the telly and a beer – just calling to him. He worried that he might feel tired if he gave up his weekends to work on the ponds.

I had to get David to see himself behaving differently.

Step 2 – App 16: Swish Bad Habits Away:
1. I asked David to make a nice big picture in his mind of him clearing out the ponds. He could see himself clearly, enjoying himself with the other volunteers.
2. Having told David to clear this picture from his mind, I then asked him to think about the very last thing he is aware of before committing himself to a day on the sofa.
3. I asked David to make sure that he is fully 'associated' when he makes this picture, i.e. he actually sees the sofa through his own eyes, rather than looking at himself. Then locate the point at which he makes that decision. What is it that he sees, what is he holding in his hands?

4. David told me he could see the TV remote in his hand. As soon as he had that, he felt tempted to switch the TV on.

5. I asked him to clear that image out of his mind again, and now call back into his mind that picture of success, of him being active down at the ponds. I told him to look at it carefully, taking in all the details.

6. I asked him to imagine this 'success picture' of his sliding out of view to his left. And to leave it here.

7. Then to call back that image of his bad habit – the one where the sofa and that TV control live.

8. To look at it closely as if he had it there in front of him.

9. Then I asked him to close his eyes and say the word '*swish*' out loud.

10. As he said this word out loud, he made his success picture quickly slide across the bad picture, pushing it out of the way completely, so he could no longer see it. His success picture came sliding across from the left-hand side, where he had placed it, and smashed straight through his 'bad-habit picture'.

11. He repeated this.

12. And repeated it again, each time placing his success picture on the left-hand side whilst having his bad-habit picture directly in front of him.

13. The more he did this, the stronger his success picture became and his bad-habit picture began to fade.

14. I asked him to finish up by taking a moment to enjoy looking at his newly installed habit.

David repeated this exercise over the next few days and when it came to the following weekend, he found it much harder to simply walk into his sitting room and place himself on that sofa. That image of the local ponds kept coming into his mind and pushed him out of the front door.

Step 3 – Cranking Up the Motivation:
Despite having been warned by his doctor that he needed to take more exercise and despite having joined the local community group, David still felt he needed an extra push to get him up and exercising.

The most logical app to download here is the Motivation Anchor – app 15. But as David's health was at stake here, I wanted to use something a little stronger to make him realise that he would only be living half a life if he did not change his habits for good:

1. I asked David to close his eyes and take himself back to the sporting moments of his life. Maybe they were pretty unremarkable, with failures on Sports Day. Did PE lessons cause him nothing but embarrassment? Was he one of the ones definitely not picked for the school team? Did he never stop wobbling on his bicycle or master the art of swimming beyond doggy paddle? Perhaps his memories were filled with times when all he did was stand at the side watching others being successful and having fun.
2. Then I asked him to open his eyes once more and become aware of the feelings that he had as a child – of missing out and being left behind.

3. I asked David to close his eyes once more and invited him to start all over again with an 'action replay' of his life. Only this time, he could have it going just the way he would have liked it to have been.

4. I asked him to imagine a TV screen in front of him, playing an action replay of his sporting childhood. If he came last on Sports Day – I asked him to have himself coming first instead. To see himself running past the fastest runner in the school. To picture himself as the strongest swimmer, swimming so fast that no one stands a chance of catching him. To be the best striker in the football team, weaving his way through the opposition, just in time to score the winning goal! This was *his* action replay and he could have it going just the way he wanted it to.

5. I told him to really enjoy watching his movie – to imagine feeling really successful, seeing what he sees, hearing what he hears and feeling how good these moments feel. I asked him to crank up the colours and increase the volume. Are there any sounds in this replay? Crowds cheering, perhaps? A parent or teacher congratulating him? I asked him to make the sounds louder.

6. I told him to keep this action replay movie of his running – his own special action replay where everything goes just the way he'd like it to have done. To make himself faster, more skilled and more successful than he ever was. Was there someone that he'd always wanted to beat? Was there a particular sport that he'd always wished he could have tried? This was his chance. I asked him to feel how good these

moments felt, as his heart began to beat a little faster. To enjoy every single moment.

7. Then I asked David to open his eyes and come back into the present moment.

We then had a moment or two for reflection. David had really enjoyed the feelings of confidence that reliving his life in that way had given him. I asked him to consider how different his life would have been if he had really been able to behave in that way.

David realised that his lack of confidence had prevented him from doing many things. Just a stupid thing like being teased at school for his lack of sporting prowess had led him to leave school early. His lack of confidence meant he hadn't applied for jobs that might have stretched him and given him the kind of rewards that he would have liked to have. And he thought of the girls that he'd been too shy to ask out. A real domino effect.

David was at a 'now or never' point in his life. Was he prepared to carry on the way he had been going and continue to miss out on life – never mind the health problems he was now facing – or could he turn things around and start exercising and losing that weight?

We worked together over the next few months and using various techniques – apps 8, 9, 10 and 15 – David turned his life around.

Case Study: Quit Smoking for Good

'More doctors smoke Camels than any other cigarette.'
Advertising slogan for Camel cigarettes 1940s–50s

Brian had been a smoker all his life. He'd always told himself that 'one day' he'd quit for good and never had he imagined that his fiftieth birthday would be staring him in the face whilst he still had a packet of cigarettes in his pocket.

Six months ago, Brian's father (also a life-long smoker) had died of lung cancer and the whole family witnessed this gruesome illness do its damage. Not wanting to create additional stress for himself at the time of his father's illness, Brian had told himself that he would give up the cigarettes for good once it was all over. After all, he was able to witness at first hand the damage that cigarettes can do to your body – surely that would be incentive enough.

As time went by, however, Brian was finding it harder and harder to quit for good. Thoughts of his father and the illness that had taken his life just seemed to make Brian want to smoke more and he couldn't quite understand why. He felt angry and ashamed of himself and, as the pressure mounted, he felt he needed something really powerful to help him.

Step 1 – App 20: Addiction Breaker: Using this exercise, I was able to attach feelings of strong repulsion to Brian's compulsion. You can use it to deal with cravings for food as well as cigarettes. As with all of these NLP techniques, take a few moments to find a quiet place where you can relax and focus.

1. I asked Brian to think about his favourite brand of cigarettes – if you are trying to quit smoking, you too can imagine a packet sitting there in front of you. Notice the colour and shape of the box and allow yourself to see a cigarette poking out of the packet invitingly.

2. After a few moments of doing this, you can wipe that imaginary picture out of your mind and create a blank space.

3. Now, think about a food that really turns your stomach. *(I chose a food item as it's something that you'd also put into your mouth.)*

4. Take a few moments to think about a time in the past when you ate something that disagreed with you and that you're adamant you'll never have again. (In Brian's case, he remembered going on a friend's stag weekend in Europe – as well as drinking too much, he'd been egged on to eat oysters. A big mistake as it turned out as they disagreed with him and the consequences were not pleasant – but perfect, as it turned out, for our purposes!)

5. Make a really big picture in front of you of that food – bringing it closer to you, turning up the colours and becoming aware of the aromas that you may even be smelling.

6. As you bring it even closer to you, just allow yourself to see your hand reach forward and place some of that food in your mouth. Open your mouth and begin to chew (actually have your mouth moving to do this), becoming aware of all the sensations of chewing that food. Notice the texture, be it rubbery and chewy or soft and squelchy.

7. And take another mouthful and chew over and over again. Keep repeating this process as you bring that plate of food closer to you still.

8. Now add another stomach-churning ingredient to that plate of food. Is there something else you could add? (In Brian's case, I added some live, wriggly maggots – and yes, invited him to eat them and continue to imagine eating them until he felt quite sick.)
9. Just as this feeling intensifies, squeeze your thumb against the two fingers you'd normally hold a cigarette in. Squeeze those fingers together and hold them there for a few moments.

Then you can imagine that plate of food getting closer and closer to you, until it feels as if it is passing right the way through you – all the way through your mouth and out through the back of your head.

How does that feel? Pretty bad, I expect. Relax those fingers now and give that hand a shake.

Now, conjure up that image of your favourite packet of cigarettes once more. See one poking out of the box and imagine taking hold of it – as you imagine holding it, once more squeeze those fingers together.

Look closely into that packet of cigarettes and you'll be able to see that stomach-churning food once more. Keep squeezing those fingers and you'll probably even be able to taste it and smell it. *(In Brian's case, he could even see the live maggots crawling out of the end of the filter.)*

If ever in the future you find yourself needing to resist the temptation to take a cigarette, eat a chocolate or a plate of chips, once you've done this exercise all you're going to have to do is squeeze your fingers together in this way and these feelings of repulsion will come flooding back to you.

Having given Brian a nasty taste in his mouth, I wanted to leave him in a more resourceful state for dealing with his habit.

Over the past few months he'd actively been trying to remember the pain and suffering his father had been through in an effort to put himself off cigarettes. It hadn't worked. All it had done was leave Brian in a lot of emotional pain. Feeling sad and empty, it was no wonder he automatically turned to nicotine to change his feelings. Cigarettes had successfully been doing this for him for many years and he didn't know of any other way.

Step 2 – Playing around with Pictures:

1. I asked Brian to roughly locate the place in front of him where he 'saw' pictures of his father when he thought about him. Brian pointed to a spot just in front of his face, out to the left-hand side. He told me he could see his father lying in a hospital bed.
2. I asked him to take that picture and move it further away. And, once he had done this, to drain the colours out slowly till the picture became black and white. And then to snap his fingers loudly and blank that picture out completely – make it vanish in an instant.
3. Without a picture to look at, Brian found the intensity of his feelings diminished.
4. Next, I asked him to remember some good times that he'd spent with his father. Brian's thoughts went back to long cricket matches and hot summers.
5. As he described the scenes he remembered, not only did a smile appear on his face, but he quickly realised that his good pictures were being made just in front of his face again, but this time over on the right-hand side.

6. I asked him to make a happy picture bigger, bring it closer to him, turn the colours up brighter and stronger. And as he did so, Brian told me he could hear his father's voice saying, 'Well done, son.'

An emotional moment, but a real breakthrough. This moment triggered a vital part of the healing process for Brian – the ability to bring positive, happy memories of a loved one to the fore, allowing the more painful ones to subside. In this more resourceful state, Brian was able to relax and say 'no' to cigarettes in a more controlled way. And each time he did so, he had his father's approval.

We all make pictures out in front of us in different locations depending on the emotions we are experiencing with that thought. Locating your place for making 'good' pictures and then your place for 'bad' pictures is a useful skill in taking control of your thoughts, rather than letting them control you.

Case Study: Compulsive Shopping

Charlotte, thirty-two, worked in a competitive and stressful environment. The hours were long and she often found herself working at weekends, but she told herself it was all worth it as she was now starting to earn a salary that outstripped those of her close friends.

We all need to let off steam now and again and Charlotte's greatest pleasure was shopping in Selfridges. Handbags, shoes, clothes, perfumes and cosmetics – it just seemed so easy to convince herself that she deserved all of this. Over the years, she'd accumulated a number of credit cards that had enabled her to just keep on going. She'd managed to successfully keep her shopping habits under wraps – until now.

A much anticipated annual bonus had failed to materialise as her firm made necessary cutbacks. Her debts had spiralled out of control and now it seemed she had no immediate way to pay them off. Some of her colleagues had been made redundant and she feared she could be next. However, the more anxious she became, the more her desire to shop increased.

Retail Therapy or Shopping Addiction?: Unlike other addictions, compulsive shoppers can get a 'high' before the actual event itself. The mere planning and anticipation of a shopping trip can bring on feelings of euphoria – nudging the person in the direction of the nearest shopping mall.

Whilst logically Charlotte could see that the happy buzz she got from shopping acted as a distraction from the stress of her work, she still felt compelled to do it.

And what usually compels someone to do something is the pictures that they're making in their minds. Charlotte had become an expert at making huge pictures of fancy shopping malls with attractive window displays. She could also clearly see herself wearing and using the things that she bought – always accompanied by a big smile on her face, of course.

What she was failing to do was make pictures of herself further down the line when the credit card bill dropped through the letter box. She was not making the connection between the shops and her debts.

Step 1 – Run the Movie to the End:

1. I invited Charlotte to take a look into her future by walking along her timeline. We elicited her timeline – App 3 – and she chose to use a ribbon laid out on the floor in front of her.

2. She oriented herself in the present moment and began to locate 'tomorrow' and then 'next week'. In fact, she had already planned a shopping trip for then, which made it all the easier for her for to see.

3. Then she looked ahead to one month down the line and then three months, followed by six months.

4. She knew she had every intention of continuing shopping throughout the next few months, regardless of what her credit card bills were telling her.

5. I asked her to begin stepping down her timeline, stopping at each of the points she had previously located and noticing what she noticed.

6. As she did this, I then invited her to walk on further – how about a year down the line? – and even further – how about two years?

7. I asked to see what she could see, hear what she could hear and feel what she could feel.

8. And then she came back down the line, all the way back to the present.

Charlotte's face said it all – she had seen things down her timeline that worried her. Whilst she knew redundancies were taking place at work and it was quite possible that it could soon be her turn, she had managed to put that picture out of her mind. Down on her timeline, though, she had encountered a view of her office and a conversation with her boss. Things had looked grim and the words that she had heard made her shudder.

We all go forward either because we feel we are moving towards something good happening or because we're moving away from something bad happening.

Charlotte admitted that whenever the negative consequences of a shopping expedition came into her mind, she quickly got rid of that image. This would need to change and she would need to keep reminding herself of the negative consequences of a shopping expedition, as this would motivate her more to keep away from the shops.

Step 2 – App 18: Negative Anchor: I asked Charlotte to think of three things that she had noticed from her walk into the future that made her feel bad.

She told me she had seen a figure appear in her mind – this figure was the amount of money she owed to credit card companies – and it was displayed in big, bold, red numbers clearly in her mind. It made her feel sick.

The second image that had come to mind was that of her boss – she could not only see him clearly but also hear him clearly as he told her that regrettably the firm would have to let her go due to cutbacks. The thought of being unemployed filled her with dread.

And third, as she had walked further along into her future she could see it being rather bleak – for some reason she saw herself living in a small bedsit rather than the nice two-bedroom flat she had at the moment. She had seen herself spending a Saturday night in as her friends had forgotten her. Not a pretty sight. Charlotte performed the following steps:

1. Charlotte closed her eyes, relaxed and allowed herself to clearly see once more the figure that represented the amount she owed. I asked her to make that picture bigger. To turn the colours up brighter and bolder and to bring it closer to her.
2. As she did this, the feelings of anxiety began to increase inside her body. I asked to imagine them becoming ten times bigger than before.
3. As the feelings intensified, she squeezed the thumb and middle finger on her **non-dominant** hand together. As she did, the feelings attached or anchored themselves to the squeezing of her fingers.
4. I asked her to release her fingers, relax and get rid of that picture.
5. Now it was time to go back to memory number two. That scene with her boss as he told her she had lost her job. She allowed herself to fully associate with this memory. She saw what she saw, heard what she heard and felt as she would feel.
6. As the feelings of anxiety grew alongside this image, she again squeezed her thumb and middle finger together, capturing all of those bad feelings there.
7. About thirty seconds later, I again asked to relax her hand and wipe that image away from her mind. For we were going on a journey elsewhere.
8. To the third memory – to that cheap, lonely bedsit of hers. A life of misery waiting for her, just a couple of years down the line.

9. Again, she intensified her feelings of anxiety by fully associating herself with this image. Making it bigger and bringing it closer to her. At the peak of her anxiety, she squeezed that thumb and middle finger together again.

10. And as she did, I asked her to notice how those bad feelings from her boss's conversation and those bad feelings from that sum of money she owed the credit card companies also came flooding back to her.

11. A real cocktail of bad, bad feelings as she squeezed that thumb and middle finger together.

Excellent work! Now Charlotte was equipped with a 'negative anchor' that she would be able to activate whenever she felt the urge to go shopping. Just to test our work out further, I invited Charlotte to take a walk down her timeline once more. As she arrived at the shopping trip she had planned for next week, I asked her to squeeze her thumb and middle fingers together once more and notice how it changed her feelings.

A Success Plan: Whilst Charlotte was now able to take control of her shopping urges and nip them in the bud, she still needed to find something to replace the buzz of good feelings that she had got from them. I reminded Charlotte that the buzz served a purpose – it was taking away her feelings of anxiety generated by work. She needed to find another way of de-stressing.

Charlotte chose exercise – she had been storing an old bicycle from her student days at her parents' house. She retrieved it and started to burn off the adrenaline caused by the stress of work by cycling through her local woods.

She took practical steps to rid herself of her debt problem too by taking advice from a financial advisor. Together they came up with a payment plan for her. Seeing it laid out in black and white made it all the easier for her to cope with.

Cas Study: In Love with Facebook

Jessie, twenty-four, had recently split up with her boyfriend and was finding it difficult to recover. They had been together for over three years and Jessie was finding it hard to adjust to life on her own. She recalled romantic drinks at the local wine bar, the flowers he used to surprise her with and, more importantly, the plans they'd started making for a future together. The break-up had been unexpected for her.

Whilst friends and family were rallying round trying to help her get over him, she still had one major problem. Each evening when she got home from work, she'd go straight onto her computer to check Facebook. However, catching up with friends also meant getting to see what her ex-boyfriend was up to. However hard she tried, she couldn't resist the temptation to check his profile and see what he was doing. Particularly upsetting were pictures he'd posted of himself at a recent party. Seeing him having so much fun made the pain much harder to bear.

Friends suggested she delete his profile, making it easier to avoid seeing what he was up to, but she hadn't quite managed to do this yet. After all, this was the one last link that she had to his life.

Step 1 – Five Moments of Horror: Jessie had given me a wonderful description of their relationship – the outings and the gifts, but I asked her to think back and tell me whether it had always been like this. Her automatic response was to say 'yes', but I asked her to pause and reflect for a moment. Could she remember five times in the past when he'd really upset her?

And so the full story began to tumble out. She could remember the time he promised her a special restaurant meal on her birthday, but then forgot to book a table. After a couple of fruitless hours searching for somewhere to eat, they ended up with fish and chips in the car.

She could remember the time they went to a party and he got really drunk and embarrassing. Not only did he insult a friend but he was also sick in the gutter on the way home. She hated the way he burped every time he drank beer.

He'd borrowed £25 from her and then denied that he'd ever had it when she asked for it back. She remembered the horrible look on his face as he accused her of lying. And she remembered the time when she caught him flirting with the barmaid at the local pub.

As I pointed out to Jessie, the reason why she was finding it so hard to get over him was because she was spending her time looking at the 'wrong movie'. Running through her mind on a daily basis was a romantic love story with her and her ex-boyfriend in the starring roles. Not only was this a slightly skewed representation of their relationship, it was also preventing her from moving on.

What she should be doing was making a new kind of movie – a

horror film – one that was made up of all the worst moments of her time together with him.

So my technique with Jessie was the following:

1. Take yourself back to that first moment of horror. See what you saw, hear what you heard and feel how fed up you felt. Run this picture through your mind again and again, making it bigger and turning the colours up brighter.
2. Move on to moment number two. And again, run that picture through your mind, doing exactly what you did with the first memory.
3. And move on – moment number three. Give it the same treatment, making that image larger and bringing it closer to you.
4. Bring moment number four quickly into mind now. Again seeing what you saw, hearing what you heard and feeling how bad this man made you feel.
5. And the last moment – run that memory through your mind.

Now take these five separate memories and run them through your mind as if they were all linked up, like a movie. There's no break between any of these situations – they all merge together. Run this horror movie through your mind, over and over again.

At the end of the technique, I asked Jessie to imagine going home and checking Facebook. How badly would she want to check his profile now?

'I don't think I can be bothered,' she replied.

Step 2 – Changing Beliefs: As the days passed, Jessie found herself thinking about her ex-boyfriend less and less – he was consigned to the past. With fewer feelings of sadness, she was able to begin looking to the future.

But as much as she wanted to feel optimistic about the prospect of meeting a new boyfriend, she just couldn't imagine it happening. She'd been with her ex for over three years – it was hard to think of herself with someone else.

Whilst everyone around her kept telling her she would be bound to meet someone soon, she was finding it hard to believe. Her ex-boyfriend had repeatedly told her that if they ever split up, she'd never find anyone else and she was beginning to worry that this might be the case.

I explained to Jessie that we needed to first of all work on the negative belief that she would never meet a new partner as it would only serve to hold her back:

1. I asked her to locate her place of strong beliefs, by thinking about something she believed in with complete certainty. Jessie had a sister – she was 100 per cent certain that she had a sister and so she thought of her.
2. She made a note of where that picture of her sister appeared and took note of the submodalities.
3. I asked her to think of something else – Jessie was certain that she'd had a tuna sandwich for lunch. Again she located that picture and made a note of the submodalities.
4. She realised that she made those two pictures in the same place – slightly to the left-hand side, right up close and in bold colours.
5. I asked her to stand up and shake herself out – to clear her mind of those pictures. And now, I asked her to think

of something she was not so certain about.

6. Jessie was not sure where she'd be going on holiday in the summertime. She hadn't thought about who she might go with or where they might go.

7. She made a hazy picture across to her right-hand side.

8. I then asked her to think about what she would be having for lunch tomorrow. She wasn't sure – perhaps a tuna sandwich again or maybe she'd meet a friend for a pizza.

9. Again, a hazy image presented itself off to her right side.

10. So we had been able to establish that she made images of things she strongly believed in to the left of her. And her uncertain thoughts popped up to the right-hand side.

11. Again I asked her to stand up and shake herself out – thus 'changing state'.

12. Now this time, I asked her to imagine herself in the future with a new boyfriend.

13. Not surprisingly, she found this a difficult picture to make and her eyes were drawn off to the right-hand side.

14. I asked her to 'pick this picture up' – to imagine transferring this hazy image of herself out with a new boyfriend – and move it across to the left-hand side. The side of complete certainty. Then, she filled in the details – added colour, sounds and feelings to the picture. And then she brought it closer to her so she could get a really close-up view of what going out with a new boyfriend looked like!

With the image in this more helpful position, Jessie's feelings about the prospect of going out and meeting a new boyfriend changed.

Step 3 – App 17: In Two Minds: Jessie was now feeling more positive about her prospects of meeting a new partner; however, getting herself up and out on dates was going to be another matter. Her confidence had been dented and she was in danger of falling into that trap of believing that because **one** boyfriend had been nasty to her, **all** boyfriends were going to be. Her mind was automatically beginning to 'generalise' and she needed to get back out on the dating scene to disprove this theory to herself.

On the one hand, she felt really excited about the prospect of having a new boyfriend but, on the other, she felt really nervous about going out and was beginning to avoid it.

I explained to Jessie that our minds are made up of various 'parts', so it's not unusual to feel in two minds about something. Whilst it may seem that the 'part' that holds us back is jeopardising our chances of success, in fact each part of us does want the best for us. The part of Jessie that was holding her back from dating was actually trying to protect her from being hurt again. Getting these two parts to come to an agreement and work together would help her to move forward:

1. I asked Jessie to stand up and have a think about these two conflicting parts inside her mind.
2. I asked her to place her hands out in front of her, elbows tucked into her sides, with her palms facing up to the ceiling.
3. I asked her to imagine that optimistic part of her in her dominant hand. She focused on the palm of her hand and could almost see a little movie being played out on it.

4. Then I asked her to imagine that nervous part of her in her non-dominant hand. Again she focused on the palm of the other hand and started to see an energy forming there.
5. I asked her to take her time and ask each part of her, in turn, what their positive intention was for her. She continued to do this until she started to recognise that, at some level, both parts wanted the same thing for her. They wanted her to be safe and happy.
6. I asked her if she could create a new 'super-part' in the space between her hands, one that could satisfy both parts of her. She looked down into the space and focused.
7. When she had done this, I asked her to quickly clasp her hands together, capturing that super-part inside her.
8. And to finish by bringing her hands right up to her chest to allow that energy to leave her hands and enter her body. She kept her hands here for a few moments as she fully absorbed the resources from the new super-part.

At the end of the exercise, Jessie reported that she felt less fearful now about venturing out and meeting new people. During the exercise, she'd had a few ideas – she decided she would keep her social life close to home, beginning to go out and socialise only with those people she knew well and trusted – her sister and her cousins came to mind – and avoiding the large nightclubs in town that were full of strangers.

Jessie helped herself further by downloading some of the other apps: App 7, Leaving the Past Behind; App 9, Creating a 'New You'; App 11, Supersize Your Confidence.

10

Fix Your Weight

The number of overweight people in the world is now outnumbering the hungry. A billion of us are now heavier than is advisable and obesity reports predict that more than half of all adults will be obese by 2050.

The more overweight people become, the more the slimming industry springs into action, creating wonder diets for us. And the more faddy diets are created, the more overweight people become. Millions of us are locked into an endless cycle of weight gain and dieting – feast and famine followed by more feast and famine.

The latest scientific research now warns us that diets can actually kill and to avoid them at all costs. But at the same time the abundance of food in our society continues to increase and opportunities to move around and burn off those calories decrease.

Rather than a new kind of diet, I believe we need to create new types of minds. Our minds shaped and moulded themselves around many years of scarce food supplies. Our habits and behaviours became fixed and are now completely inappropriate for our lifestyles and the abundance of food available to us.

We need to be taking control of our eating habits through our minds, for what's going on inside your mind is more important than what's on your plate.

Losing weight with NLP is not like any other diet, for the focus is on changing eating habits and your relationship with food, rather than on counting calories or denying yourself. As soon as we begin using labels such as 'good foods' and 'bad foods', we are setting ourselves up for failure. On a conventional diet you will sooner or later find yourself eating a 'bad food', for sometimes it's just not possible to avoid them. This is the point at which the struggles begin and people find themselves in a downward spiral. Using NLP means you'll never be put in that situation, for what is controlled is your hunger signals, cravings and self-image, rather than the food.

Over the years, I've worked with hundreds of clients and I know the pitfalls of trying to lose weight. I'm going to deal with those recurring issues here and show you how you can gain back control over your mind, rather than allowing it to continue running out of control.

Plus, I'll be showing you how to apply a hypnotic gastric band. Yes, really: it's possible to shrink your stomach through your mind. I often hear even slightly overweight people say they wish they could have a gastric band fitted. Most of us, though, don't have enough weight to lose to be considered for bariatric surgery: the costs and risks would far outweigh the potential benefits. But the idea is tempting – 'If only my stomach could shrink in size then I wouldn't be able to eat so much.'

The hypnotic gastric band is an imaginary band and not a real one, so it's not necessary to be several stones overweight to follow this procedure. And you can keep it on for as long or as little as you like. When you feel you've had enough, you can remove it.

If you'd like to 'download' the gastric band app, it's best to follow all the steps in this chapter first, plus all the apps relating to weight loss, and then use the DIY Band technique at the end. Alternatively, you can purchase the CD from my website, www.aliciaeaton.co.uk

But first, I have to remind you that you are working with these techniques through a book and not in a face-to-face session. When clients come to see me, I make sure they are fully prepared before we move on to the NLP techniques. So you'll have to be doing this for yourself.

If you're really serious about controlling your weight, go back to Chapter 7, 'Goal!', follow the instructions and make sure you have a really clear idea of what it is you're aiming to achieve.

Remember too that our habits are all connected with each other and trying to break one (i.e. overeating) can create a little bit of resistance, so it's best to change a few habitual patterns of behaviour at the same time. Follow the steps in Chapter 9.

Make sure that you're nice and relaxed before downloading any apps and that you're doing the visualisation exercises by

---

Remember This

Preparation is 90 per cent of success.

working through the techniques in Chapter 8, 'Get in the Right State'.

And finally, if you're really serious about wanting to lose weight – never give up. An obvious and simple piece of advice, I know, but in my years of working with clients, this is the one area that continues to surprise me. The speed with which people give up.

If the extra weight you're carrying went onto your body over a number of years, it's not going to drop off in a couple of days or weeks. You will not succeed if you give up. Stick with it and success will come your way. In this book you will find a whole variety of apps for your mind to download, so there's no excuse for getting fed up – do something different each day.

Let's start losing weight now.

I've Had Enough of This

To begin with, I'd like you to remember a time in the past when your weight caused you real discomfort and distress:

- Perhaps you can remember a time when you felt embarrassed as you undressed on a crowded beach.

- Or did you perhaps catch sight of your reflection in a shop window and felt pretty unhappy with what you saw.

- Or maybe you can remember a time when you overate and felt truly stuffed and sick.

- Remember that time when someone told you you're fat?

- And what about the time you felt ten times more fed up with your weight than you ever had before as you looked in the mirror.

Rather than forgetting these moments, I'd like you to remember them vividly. Make a note on a piece of paper of the five worst memories you can come up with. The next steps are an eyes-closed process, so read through all the instructions first before you attempt to do them. Or ask a friend to read the instructions out loud for you.

1. I'd like you to close your eyes and remember the first memory. Run it through your mind, making the picture even bigger and the sounds even louder. Remember the situation and remember the feeling.

2. Move on to the second episode and again run it through your mind. Make the colours brighter, bolder, stronger and the sounds louder as you turn the volume up. And notice your feelings – make them spin ten times faster.

3. And now take that third memory of yours. Do exactly the same as before and make that picture bigger and bring it closer to you.

4. And now the fourth episode.

5. And now the fifth, doing exactly the same as before, making those pictures bigger, brighter, bolder and closer.

Take each scenario one by one and run it through your mind in the same way, making a clear picture of what exactly happened to make you feel so, so bad.

Then start running the episodes through your mind a little faster – joining them all up as if they were a movie.

Your very own disaster movie! And say the words out loud: 'I've had enough of this! I've had enough of this! I've had enough of this!'

Enough already! Yes, I think you've suffered enough now. Hopefully you have a very clear idea now of exactly **why** you'd like to lose some weight.

How many years of your life have you wasted by being overweight? And how many more years are you going to put up with this?

Exercise: Need More Convincing?

I'm going to invite you to take a walk into your future. Before carrying out this visualisation exercise, you'll need to have used some of the relaxation techniques in Chapter 8.

Read through this exercise, then close your eyes and allow your mind to drift. Better still, ask a friend to guide you through this meditation. Take around fifteen minutes for this.

1. Imagine yourself walking along a pathway in a meadow. Notice the trees, the flowers and the sunshine.

2. As you walk along, you notice a fork in the road. You choose to go off to the right.

3. As you do, you notice a signpost – it reads 'The Path of No Change'.

4. As you continue to walk along this path, you notice a shadowy figure up ahead.

5. The figure begins to call out to you – 'Come closer, come closer. I have something to tell you.'

6. You walk closer and realise that this shadowy figure is in fact *you*. You've walked into the future – it's ten years from now.

7. You realise that this person is the 'you' who chose to continue over-eating and putting on weight.

8. 'I have something to tell you,' the figure says. 'Come closer.'

9. You walk closer and take a good look at this person who is now ten years older and very much heavier.

10. Listen carefully to their words. Listen now. Pause.

11. When you have finished listening to what it is they wanted to tell you, thank them, turn around and walk back down the pathway until you find yourself back at the fork in the road.

12. Now you decide to walk along the path that leads off to the left.

13. As you walk along this path, you see a signpost that reads 'The Path of Positive Change'.

14. As you continue to walk along this path, you notice a shadowy figure up ahead once more.

15. The figure begins to call out to you: 'Come closer, come closer. I have something to tell you.'

16. You walk closer and you realise that this shadowy figure is in fact *you*. You've walked into the future. It's ten years from now.

17. But this time, you realise that this person is the 'you' who chose to get to grips with the problem and lose all that extra weight.

18. 'I have something to tell you,' the figure says. 'Come closer.'

19. You walk closer and take a good look at this person who is now ten years older but very much lighter and more confident.

20. Listen carefully to their words. Listen now. Pause.

21. When you have finished listening to what it is they wanted to tell you, thank them for their wisdom, turn around and walk back down the pathway until you find yourself back at the fork in the road.

22. Here you can pick up that main path once more and follow it back down to the meadow.

23. Everything looks just as it did when you first set out on your journey.

24. Open your eyes and come back into the room.

Take some time to reflect on what you learnt from this exercise.

The Secret Habits of Naturally Thin People

One of the most important principles for successful behaviour that the development of NLP has been able to demonstrate is that you need to know what 'success' looks like. Too many of us know exactly what we *shouldn't* be doing if we want to lose weight. But how many of us have a clear idea of what exactly we *should* be doing?

The concept of modelling is perhaps where NLP started. The originators looked at other people's behaviours and discovered that, if they copied them exactly, they too could achieve similar results.

So in order to become a slimmer, healthier person it's important to begin by looking at the habits of naturally slim people. What is it that they do exactly? And what are you going to have to 'model' in order to become just like them? Naturally slim people:

1. Trust their bodies to regulate their weight for them. They know that if they've overeaten on holiday, their bodies will bring them back to their normal weight – they don't panic by going on a diet.

2. Know intuitively what to eat: if they feel the need to eat chocolate, they do so. Avoiding certain foods and labelling them as 'bad' will result in cravings.

3. Know intuitively how much to eat. Naturally thin people stop eating before they get completely full. They're happy to leave food on their plates without feeling guilty.

4. Eat when they are hungry but sometimes also eat when they are not. They can differentiate between a physical need and a physical desire. They recognise when a treat is just a treat and don't incorporate it into their everyday behaviour.

5. Deal with their emotional hunger in ways that don't involve food. They have other strategies at their disposal.

6. Have a positive self-image. This is not just in relation to their size and shape but in relation to other aspects of their lives too.

Hunger Signals

Too often it becomes easy to lose touch with our real hunger signals. Start recognising all the other reasons why you may have a feeling inside your body that you describe as 'hunger':

- **Boredom**: Are you in the middle of a repetitive task or perhaps have nothing to do?

- **Stress**: Are you thinking about a difficulty or a problem?

- **Anger:** Are you replaying an argument or stressful situation in your mind?

- **Loneliness:** Could you do with a chat or meeting up with friends?

- **Tiredness**: Eating food won't make you feel any less tired.

- **Pain**: A very common reason for overeating that's often overlooked.

- **Frustration**: What else could you be doing to solve your difficulty?

- **Deep in concentration**: Keep food away from TVs and computers.

Exercise: Take a Look Around

If you'd like a little more evidence that it's possible to learn how to behave like a naturally thin person and so become one, try this exercise when you are next eating in a restaurant or coffee bar (or even in a burger bar – after all, thin people eat there too!):

1. Have a good look around the restaurant and see if you can spot some thin people eating and drinking. And notice the following:
    - The speed at which they are eating.
    - Do they put their knife and fork (or burger) down in between mouthfuls?
    - Do they chew their food many times over?
    - Do they chat to others during the course of the meal?
    - Are they happy to leave some food on their plates?
    - Do they appear to be relaxed?

2. Now you can repeat this observation watching the habits of overweight people and notice how they differ.

Take a few moments now to think about your own style of eating – would it be more like the thin people or the overweight ones? And what changes could you make for the better?

Work through the apps in this book and see what other more helpful solutions you could find for your problems.

As another guideline – real hunger gets registered in the body gradually. It begins with a gentle, empty feeling that continues to build up over a period of half an hour. Imagined hunger, on the other hand, often strikes suddenly as a desire to eat that simply pops into our minds out of nowhere. This type of hunger is the brain's desire for a 'change of scenery'. Placing food on the tongue sends an instant message up to the brain, exciting a different part of it, quite literally taking our mind 'off' things, which makes us feel relaxed and happier.

What Do I Really Want?: Remember, too, that if you've become accustomed to answering every signal and message that your brain sends you with a bite to eat, then you're never really listening to what your body is telling you. And as a result, you're never really responding to those signals in the right way.

People who feel bored and irritated by their jobs will stuff their faces with snacks all day, sometimes never realising that what they should really be doing is perhaps taking on a more interesting or challenging role elsewhere.

Many people who live alone eat throughout the day without realising that their body's desire to move its mouth is more a need for conversation than food. Picking up the phone and seeking out some company would be a better bet.

Each time you place a piece of food in your mouth when you are not really hungry, then it's not only another occasion when you are literally making your body larger, but yet another occasion when you are missing out on doing whatever it is the 'inner you' would really like to be doing. How much longer are you going to be content with missing out? Life is short – it would be good to start right now.

Pay Attention!

If you can't properly pay attention to your body's signals when you are eating, you will gradually become one of those people who is never quite sure when they are hungry and when they are not. I say 'become' because as children we are born with a natural ability to recognise the signs of hunger and fullness.

Eating consciously is going to be the key to losing weight. So what is conscious eating *not*?

- It's not in front of the TV.

- It's not standing up.

- It's not in the car, on the bus or walking down the street.

Conscious eating is not eating crisps straight out of the packet, because as your hand disappears into the packet and then moves straight up to your mouth, you don't get a chance to see the food itself. And if you can't see it, as far as your brain is concerned, it just didn't happen.

The best example of unconscious eating has to be in a dark cinema where everyone stares at the screen as their hands disappear into their tubs of popcorn. Ever got half-way through a movie and been surprised to find your tub completely empty? And have you ever then turned and glared at the person sitting next to you, convinced that they must have helped themselves to your popcorn when you weren't looking? Yes – that's unconscious eating.

Make a Meal of a Meal: We know that 'hunger' can occur in the brain without a real sense of hunger in the stomach. We talk about emotional hunger – hunger in the head rather than the stomach.

It is our brains that do the 'feeling' bit for our bodies. Because of advances in psychological knowledge, we now know, for example, that 'phantom limb pain' is something that is genuinely experienced by people who have lost a limb. Strange to think, but it is possible to feel an itch on an arm or leg that's no longer there. It's our brains that do the 'feeling'.

And in just the same way, it's not only our stomachs that experience a sense of fullness when we've been eating – but also our brains. Which is why if you've been eating in front of the TV or in the car or on the run, your brain won't have registered it in quite the same way as if you had eaten consciously. I always tell my clients 'make a meal of a meal'.

Aim for an all-round sensory hit, exciting each and every one of your senses. Make the table as attractive as possible: colourful napkins, attractive cutlery and crockery. How about some flowers or maybe a candle?

And what about the food – the colours, textures and aromas? The more exciting and stimulating to your senses of sight, touch, taste and smell, I guarantee the more satisfied you'll feel and the easier it will be to experience that feeling of fullness on less food.

If you're listening to your iPod or texting your friends at the same time as eating, I can also guarantee that the food won't make the slightest impact.

Variety is the Spice of Life: Shepherd's pie on Wednesdays, sausages on Thursdays, fish on Fridays.

Does this sound familiar to you? Without even realising, families who follow repetitive patterns of eating are also encouraging unconscious eating. Nobody questions, nobody asks – without even thinking about it, everyone eats the same thing each week. And if you get used to eating the same food, you very quickly get used to eating the same quantity regardless of whether you need it or not. Unconscious eating *never* leads to a feeling of fullness and satisfaction – only a desire for more food.

So if you find yourself craving food even when you know you're not hungry – check back to your last meal. How exciting was it? Life in the twenty-first century is so much brighter, louder and more stimulating than just fifty years ago – our mealtimes need to be the same.

Your Success Strategy

The habits of naturally slim people can be analysed and translated into a success strategy that you too can follow:

1. Always respond to an initial hunger signal with a glass of water and wait ten minutes to see if your 'hunger' was in fact thirst.

2. Only eat in response to a real hunger signal – not an imagined one, and get to grips with recognising the difference. Download App 19.

3. Keep a sticker on the fridge: 'What do I really want?' Remember each time you eat food when you're not really hungry is just one more of those occasions when you're not getting what you really, really want or need.

4. Eat consciously and slowly. Act like a gourmet and go to town by 'making a meal of a meal'.

5. Stop eating as soon as you get a full signal – use your Negative Anchor App 18 if you need something to help you put the brakes on.

6. Don't force yourself to eat foods that are 'slimming' if you don't like them – you'll trigger cravings when you're not really hungry. Really enjoy the food you do eat.

7. Eat off a smaller-sized plate and get into the habit of always leaving something uneaten on it.

Body Image

Looking in a mirror is often a baby's favourite activity, as we are naturally drawn to the sight of a human face. This fascination usually continues through middle childhood – as children we love looking at ourselves, dancing around, singing with hair-brushes in our hands and pulling faces in the mirror. At this stage of our lives, we're often imploring adults to 'look at me'.

It doesn't take too many more years, however, for most of us to want to avoid looking in the mirror as what we see fails to live up to our ideals. Psychologists define body image as 'a person's thoughts, perceptions and feelings about their body'. This means that when you look in a mirror, what you actually see is your perception of how you look rather than the 'real' image that others see.

Fortunately there are ways of making friends with your image in the mirror by using a well-known NLP technique. As well as using it regularly with my own clients, I've also had a great deal of experience of using this many times over when assisting at Paul McKenna's Weight Loss Seminars. At these events, it's not uncommon to have 500 people attending, and working as an assistant has often resulted in my having twenty to thirty delegates to work with in quick succession in front of a mirror.

Each delegate would begin by telling me what it is they do not like about themselves when they look in a mirror.

This often starts in the usual way with common responses being 'my fat thighs, my big stomach . . .' What surprised me, however, is how quickly this would escalate into a torrent of personal abuse of themselves

It is a fact that you are your harshest critic. And the more you criticise yourself, the more you will allow others to do the same. So if you often find yourself being criticised by other people, just take a few minutes to stop, reflect and become aware of how much you criticise yourself. Perhaps it's time to raise the bar – quite literally, the nicer you are to yourself, the nicer others will be to you.

On the seminars, the personal criticism was often about things that people could not change: 'I hate the colour of my eyes' is a common example, and 'I wish I was taller'. The fact is that when these delegates looked into the mirrors they were not looking at reflections of their bodies, but at reflections of their thoughts and feelings.

Many studies have shown that higher levels of self-esteem help to inoculate you against dissatisfaction with body shape. Which is why working on yourself 'on the inside' is what will help you to feel better about 'the outside'.

Some people feel this means they have to learn to love the less attractive bits of themselves and are reluctant to do this. But accepting your body shape and the bits of you that cannot be changed is more about seeing yourself as others see you. We all know people who despite their larger size always look happy, confident and very attractive.

My advice is to learn to love the bits you cannot change and

> ### Remember This
> *Feel good on the inside and it will show on the outside.*

do something about the ones that you can. It's possible to go through life never truly being happy with yourself, and remember, this will only result in more unhappiness – what you focus on, you get more of. Download App 23 to get over your fear of the mirror.

Case Study: Mistaken Hunger

Julia, forty-two, had been on and off diets for pretty much the last five years. Although she did go through periods of losing weight it was all too easy to put that weight back on. This continual yo-yoing had put her completely out of touch with her body and its true needs. She felt the only way to break through this problem was to start listening to her body rather than reading instructions from a diet magazine.

Julia felt she had completely lost her 'full' and 'empty' hunger signals – she was always hungry, she told me. And then five minutes later she told me she was never really hungry as she snacked throughout the day. Not only was she confused in her mind, she was confused in her body.

Step 1 – App 19: Recalibrating Hunger Signals: I helped Julia to solve this problem by showing her how to become consciously aware of what both states felt like once more. You can do the same by downloading App 19. You can run through this exercise several times and soon you'll begin to get to grips with your body's real and imagined 'hungry' signals and be able to respond in the appropriate way.

Julia enjoyed working as part of a team in a large accounts department – whilst she'd made good friends there, the work could sometimes seem tedious and repetitive. Certain times of the year were worse than others, particularly the end of the financial year. As she left the office at the end of the day to walk to the bus stop, she would pass a newsagent's that had a small fridge in the corner with sandwiches in it.

Every day she would pop in, buy a sandwich and eat it whilst waiting at the bus stop. By her own admission, they were not great sandwiches – packaged in plastic, they were lunchtime leftovers. She also wasn't really sure that she was hungry when she left the office, but somehow those sandwiches were just calling out to her and she felt unable to resist. She would arrive home feeling full but would still have to prepare the family's meal and sit down and eat with them. She was eating too much and wanted to eliminate the sandwiches but didn't know where to begin. She wanted to get control of making decisions, but each day she was making a bad one – buying the sandwich.

Julia had told me that she bought a sandwich 'every day' – I started by asking her if this was true. She thought about it and realised that some days she walked to the bus stop with a couple of her workmates – on these days, she avoided the sandwiches as she was just too busy chatting.

It's easy to fall into the trap of believing that we make our 'bad decisions' a split second before our actions. But in fact, Julia was making her bad decision long before she left the office. I asked her to work backwards and make a list of everything she did leading up to that sandwich purchase. It looked something like this:

1. Purchase sandwich.
2. Select sandwich.
3. Walk to fridge cabinet.
4. Enter newsagent's.
5. Walk down high street.
6. Walk down side street.
7. Leave office building.
8. Catch lift from fourth floor to ground.
9. Say goodbye to workmates.
10. Collect bags.
11. Put on overcoat.
12. Switch off computer.
13. Tidy desk.
14. Work finishes 5 p.m.

I asked Julia again about those days when she left the office with some of her colleagues and for her to try to elaborate on why she didn't buy a sandwich on those days. She told me they were usually too busy laughing and joking to eat.

On the days she left the office alone, she often felt tired and weary and in need of a pick-me-up. She could quickly see that she felt better if she left the office in the company of friends, but wasn't always possible to all leave at the same time. When they could, it was a bonus.

Laughter has a powerful effect on our brain chemistry: it releases endorphins, those feelgood chemicals. Feeling tired at the end of a busy day working at a computer screen, for Julia laughing with her colleagues was a good way of shuffling around her brain chemistry, making her feelings of 'hunger' much less obvious.

Whilst Julia wasn't always going to be able to control who she walked to the bus stop with at the end of each day, she could take control of her body's neuro-physiology in other ways. Tracking back through her movements leading up to the sandwich purchase, I suggested she avoided taking the lift to the ground floor and jogged down those four flights of stairs instead. As well as the benefits of using up calories, the exercise would have the same effect as the laughing with friends and release those feelgood chemicals. Julia quickly came to realise that her sandwich cravings were really her body's way of calling out for that change of scenery at the end of a busy day.

Rather than gritting your teeth and relying on willpower to handle temptation for you, backtrack through your bad decision-making process and see how much further back you need to go to discover what drives your unwanted behaviour.

Step 2 – App 16: Swish Bad Habits Away: Changing habits that have become an automatic way of behaving for us can be tricky. A thought pops into your mind and before you have time to be consciously aware of it, you are already responding in a way that you would rather not.

Julia quickly realised that whilst the sandwich purchase was a bad decision for her, there was no reason why she shouldn't still reward herself at the end of the day. She decided to swap the sandwich for a magazine instead.

As most of us are aware, despite our best intentions we don't always end up behaving in the way that we would like. To erase the bad patterns of behaviour and install a new, more positive behaviour, I used the NLP swish pattern with Julia.

Before you download this app, decide which new behaviour you will be using to take the place of the old behaviour.

Case Study: Bored with Eating

Nicole, thirty-two, came to see me for help with her eating habits. She didn't need to lose a great deal of weight – half a stone at the most – but she told me she often experienced cravings for food in the evening even though she knew she'd eaten enough earlier and wasn't really hungry. It was this feeling of being out of control around food in the evenings that she wanted to deal with.

Looking at her problem more closely I discovered that she often ate just a plate of plain pasta with a knob of butter for dinner – she told me she wasn't a fussy eater and was quite happy with this, and as she lived alone she could please herself.

But although she may have been happy with this, her brain clearly wasn't. Hence the cravings. The lack of colour, aroma and variety in texture meant her brain was left screaming out for some stimulation. In addition, she also told me that she ate in front of the TV – so her brain never got to 'see' the plate of food either!

For a long time, Nicole had thought the solution to her problem was *not* to think about food, but I was able to encourage her to do the exact opposite. By literally 'making a meal' of her mealtimes, as well as choosing really exciting foods to eat, she found consuming fewer calories easier than she had done for years. By acting like a gourmet, she became more adventurous in her tastes and developed a more discerning palate. She quickly discovered that the pickier and fussier she became about the quality of her food, making sure to include plenty of protein, the less likely she was to treat herself as a dustbin.

Step 1 – App 25: Reversing Hunger Pangs: I used a variation of App 25, Reversing Feelings of Anxiety. Whilst Nicole's feelings were not anxious ones, spinning her hunger pangs in the opposite direction saved her from those second helpings and unnecessary snacks.

1. The next evening at home, Nicole was experiencing her usual cravings. I had instructed her to use her index finger to point to where those feelings were inside her and to track the direction in which they were moving.
2. She discovered that her feelings were moving in quite a thin line, from the bottom of her stomach and rising up to her throat. *(Note – not all of us experience these types of feelings in the same way, so yours could move differently.)*
3. They then felt as if they came out of her mouth and went back down into the bottom of her stomach again. Once more that feeling would travel from her stomach, up through her body into her mouth and out again.
4. It was like a circle – the feelings were going round and round.
5. I asked her if she could give these feelings a colour. Interestingly, she chose purple – a colour often associated with chocolate.

6. Adding a colour made it easier for Nicole to visualise the next steps.

7. I asked her to imagine pulling those feelings out of her body and holding them out in front of her – that hoop of purple feelings.

8. She then flipped it around, so it was now facing in the opposite direction.

9. I asked her to insert those feelings back inside her.

10. To her delight, the feelings now started to spin in the opposite direction. So instead of rising up towards her mouth, they were sliding back down towards her stomach.

11. As they reached her stomach, they would leave her body and travel back round in a circle until they reached her mouth once more. And then travelled back down again.

12. Interestingly, Nicole reported that the colour had changed too. No longer purple, the feelings were now a pale green.

This is a valuable way of stemming those imaginary feelings of hunger and is particularly effective if you need to use it in restaurants when being offered dessert.

For Nicole, creating that break in her feelings gave her valuable moments in which to make a better decision. Rather than eating, she chose to telephone her friends in the evenings.

We then worked together to treat her real 'hunger' needs, which were not only to do with boredom, but also the tediousness of living and eating alone.

She downloaded Apps 9, 10 and 11 to work on her self-image and Apps 19, 20, 21 to work with her eating habits.

Case Study: Virtual Gastric Band

Peter came to see me because he'd been struggling with his weight for the past fifteen years. He was now 52. By his own admission he'd always been on the large side, but things had now spiralled out of control. Life had just got too busy – he had a wife and three children, a large mortgage to pay off, a job with long hours and any opportunity to take exercise had simply vanished.

Over the years he had tried various diets and the inevitable yo-yoing of losing weight and gaining weight had begun. It seemed as if every diet he came across promised that he'd look good in a bikini – something he had no intention of ever wearing! – and he was struggling to find a weight-loss system that a man could identify with.

However, he was now six stone overweight, with high blood pressure and creaky knees, and the doctors had told him that he was staring diabetes in the face. He had to take action and had come to the conclusion that there just are no miracle diets and that he would have to take a different route.

We worked together over a period of two and a half years. That may sound like a long time but Peter's persistence paid off. For the first month we had weekly sessions and then reduced these to twice a month for the next three months. We then reduced the frequency down to once every six weeks, when Peter would come for a 'top-up' and looked upon these sessions as his opportunity to de-stress himself.

There was no magical 'quick fix' and at times Peter's weight plateaued for a month or so. I pointed out to him that hitting a plateau should not be considered a bad thing but actually a very useful period during which the mind is able to register the body's 'new normal'. Our minds create a mental map of our bodies and if your body is changing quickly, it can take a while for your mind to catch up. It's not uncommon for people to lose weight and then discover that their minds drag them back to what it considers to be their normal weight and size. Visualisation exercises under hypnosis are very useful during this phase – getting the mind and body to synchronise.

Peter did go on to reach his target weight – a weight he hadn't been at for many years. But more importantly, the programme had not only changed his eating habits but his entire life.

Peter's 'Gastric Band': It was several weeks before we got to the stage of fitting the hypnotic gastric band. First, Peter needed to have a clear idea of the programme he should follow and train himself to eat only when hungry and stop when he felt the tiniest bit full. He developed new routines and skills by learning all the NLP weight-loss techniques. His sessions under hypnosis enabled him to see himself clearly in the future as a slimmer, fitter, healthier person.

1. On the day of Peter's 'operation', he came into the room and we began work straight away. I kept the conversation to a minimum as Peter knew he had come in for his procedure. The room had been prepared in advance – the smell of antiseptic filled the air and a CD played hospital sound effects. A golf ball and a wide elastic band were placed by the side of the bed.

2. Peter lay down and I relaxed him by putting him into a light trance. I began by guiding him through App 21, Snack Attack, as I wanted him to be reminded of the cause of his problem. He visualised all the excess food and snacks that he had been consuming on a daily basis for many years.

3. With Peter feeling ashamed and repulsed, I asked him to squeeze his hand into a tight fist. I reminded him that this was about the size of his stomach.

4. Then I asked him to think about all the food that he had seen on that conveyor belt. To ask himself how it all ever managed to fit in – no wonder at times he had felt pretty unwell. I gave him a few moments to take this in.

5. Then I asked him to open his hand and I placed the golf ball in it. I told him to squeeze it tightly to get a good feel for its size. This is how small the human stomach becomes after it has had a surgical gastric band fitted.

6. As he continued to clench that golf ball in his hand, I took the elastic band and wrapped it around his hand as many times as it would stretch.

7. Then I asked him to bring his hand over his stomach and rest it there.

8. I then asked him to picture his stomach shrinking down to the size of that ball. We know that the mind has a powerful effect on the body and I told him to keep seeing his stomach shrinking down, smaller and smaller.

9. And now to see a band, as tight as the one wrapped around his hand, being fitted around his stomach. I pushed his

clenched fist with the elastic band round it hard into his stomach (he had given me permission to do this beforehand).

10. I gave him a five minutes to fully adjust to this shrinking stomach of his and the tightness he would feel around it from now on.

11. Then I invited him to open his eyes and come back into the room. I told him he could remove the elastic band from around his hand, but to put it (not too tightly) over his wrist instead.

12. As long as Peter keeps wearing this band around his wrist, he'll discover that small amounts of food will easily satisfy him from now on.

13. I told him that should he ever find himself eating more than is necessary, to snap the band hard around his wrist and the tight feeling would act as a reminder of the procedure his stomach had undergone. The sensation would put him back in control once more.

The operation had a powerful effect on Peter and fitting it a few weeks after he had begun his weight-loss programme meant he avoided that inevitable slow down of weight loss that's common with conventional diets.

Six weeks later, we repeated the operation and Peter had the band tightened once more. Towards the end of his programme, it was removed altogether.

11

Fix Your Confidence

Confidence can be one of the most difficult qualities to fake. We've all met people whose 'insides' don't match their 'outsides' as their boastfulness, name-dropping and expensive accessories highlight rather than disguise their shortcomings.

As you've already discovered, your mind is extraordinarily powerful, as your thoughts determine almost everything that happens to you. Perhaps one of the most important psychological discoveries is that *we become what we think about most of the time*. It's possible to 'think' yourself confident by exercising your brain in the right way, on a daily basis.

You Need to Get Out More

It's not uncommon for our lives to seemingly shrink as we get older. After the initial burst of friendships formed at school and university, grown-up life begins to take its toll. As the demands of work and family eat into our time, we can quickly find ourselves living in the same place and in the same way for many years. Breaking out from this pattern can seem not only too big an effort, but also quite intimidating.

Discovering new hobbies, meeting new people and generally being open-minded and adventurous can not only help us to become more confident, but also inoculate us from future stresses. Building up a resilience protects you and enables you to bounce back more easily from setbacks such as job losses and relationship breakdowns. So keeping up your confidence levels can be good for your health!

Answer these questions to see if you need to get out more. During the last six months how often did you:

☐ Initiate conversations with strangers?

☐ Spend time having a deep discussion with someone with radically different political or religious views?

☐ Watch television programmes that weren't on your list of favourites?

☐ Buy or read a different newspaper or magazine from the one that you usually read?

☐ Experiment with a different type of cooking?

☐ Visit a place that you have never seen before?

☐ Read a book by an author previously unknown to you?

☐ See a film (or go to a show or concert, etc.) that wasn't a 'safe bet' for you?

☐ Spend a few social hours in the company of people with very different jobs from yourself?

☐ Spend extended periods of time with people of a different generation from yourself (other than your immediate family)?

☐ Find yourself plagued by the 'travel bug' and wishing you had more time to get to know new places?

☐ Feel curious and fascinated by the customs and rituals of people from other cultures?

☐ Take an active step towards gaining more information and understanding about another culture or a different philosophy?

Make a list of actions you could take to broaden your horizons and develop your ability to empathise with other people. For example:

• Join a class or club that gives you opportunities for discussions with people from different backgrounds and cultures.

• Start saving for a different kind of holiday.

• Watch one different kind of television programme per week.

• Join a drama group to 'get into the shoes' of other people.

• Read more novels and autobiographies.

• Enquire about doing some voluntary work.

What is Shyness?

One of the most commonly asked questions about shyness is, 'Are we born shy?' The answer to that question has to be 'no'. Shyness can be described as a feeling of apprehension or awkwardness experienced in new situations or with unfamiliar people. There are three main reasons why this feeling occurs: 1) excessive self-consciousness, 2) excessive negative self-evaluation and 3) excessive negative self-preoccupation.

All three characteristic features of shyness involve a sense of self and psychological studies have shown that the 'sense of self' – our self-awareness – does not develop until we reach the age of eighteen months.

Learning how to take the 'attention, focus and awareness' off yourself and onto your surroundings and the other people is the key to feeling relaxed and confident.

And if you think shyness is merely a social inconvenience, think again. According to researchers at Chicago's Northwestern University, who carried out a thirty-year study, shy types are 50 per cent more likely to suffer a heart attack or stroke as a result of the stressfulness of new situations. They are also more susceptible to viral infections such as the common cold.

'It seems like sensitive people are simply wired to respond to stress more strongly than resilient people,' says Bruce Naliboff, one of the research authors.

It would appear, then, that tackling your shyness can not only be good for your social life, but also your health!

Top Tips for Overcoming Shyness in Social Situations:

1. Be one of the first guests to arrive – get there early. Now if this advice sounds like the complete opposite of anything you'd ever dream of doing, you'll be on your way to discovering why social situations haven't always gone the way you'd like them to. Arriving a few minutes early means you may be the first to arrive, allowing you to help out with last-minute preparations and be an extra pair of hands in the kitchen or organising a cloakroom. When other guests begin to arrive, you'll have the opportunity to meet them a few at a time and start conversations more easily. Contrast this with arriving later when you're required to walk into a party that's in full swing. Getting into conversations at this point often means joining a group that's already established, which is very much harder.

2. As soon as you are introduced to someone, use their name when responding – 'Nice to meet you . . .'. Not only will this help you to remember their name for the future but people feel flattered when their names are used in conversation and you'll connect better with them.

3. Mirror their actions – remember the rapport skills you were able to build up in Chapter 5, 'S-T-R-E-T-C-H' Your Mind.

4. Attend functions that suit your temperament and interests. It's not essential that you enjoy loud music and parties if you feel happier at art galleries and musical recitals. If you prefer wearing casual clothes to the more

formal variety, choose to attend social events that enable you to do this.

5. Rather than worrying about possible topics of conversation with complete strangers, aim to keep your small talk very small to begin with – e.g. smile and say 'hello' to as many people as you want to make eye contact with. Ask for directions to the cloakrooms or the food. Give sincere compliments – 'That's a pretty dress.' Or offer assistance by holding doors open for people. This will enable you to get used to talking with people that you do not know.

6. Make a point of listening to news items and reading a few newspapers before the event so you're up on current topics – these need not be heavy news items – quirky, humorous items or a piece of celebrity gossip will be sufficient. It's very likely that other people at the event will also be aware of this story and you'll be able to feel 'connected' as you share this knowledge.

7. Remember, other people feel shy too! Rather than worrying how you're going to muscle in on other people's conversations or join a group, look around the outskirts of the room. Identify those hanging around at the side, looking lonely. Approach them and introduce yourself. They'll be delighted to see you as you will have rescued them from embarrassing loneliness and they'll welcome your presence with open arms.

Case Study: Into the Big Wide World

Rebecca came to see me just after sitting her A-levels at school. Life was about to change for her with a university place in the pipeline and the prospect of a summer job. Whilst she felt confident in her studies, branching out and meeting new people was starting to worry her.

She was struggling to make the transition from her schoolgirl environment to the adult world. She had been asked to attend a group interview for a summer job and she told me that she feared that as soon as she saw the other applicants, she would immediately clam up and be lost for words. And even worse, if she did open her mouth to speak she just knew that her face and neck would turn bright red.

I told Rebecca that she was doing exactly the right thing in planning for the event, as there were a number of things she could do to help herself both before and during it. Pitching up on the day and just hoping things will go well isn't a successful enough strategy in this day and age. I created a step-by-step programme for her to follow in order to prepare herself.

Step 1 – Live in the Moment: Rebecca's mind was running away with her, creating doom-and-gloom scenarios of events that had yet to happen. She was predicting the future and, if she carried on doing this, her body would quite literally follow the instructions that her mind was giving it. I suggested that Rebecca practise 'living in the moment' and fully associating herself with her environment. I asked her to practise by taking a ten-minute walk each day and describing to herself what she saw. For example

– that tree has very green leaves and I can see a large brown dog running across the grass.

Transferring her attention to outside herself in this way would mean that her internal dialogue would be less likely to feed her with negative thoughts. When she found herself sitting in that interview situation, she'd be able to notice her surroundings – there's a large plant in the corner of the room, the carpet is blue with a patterned stripe, etc. – which would take the place of her usual internal dialogue which would probably be comparing her (most unfavourably) to the other candidates sitting next to her.

Step 2 – Relax: Rebecca had told me that she suffered feelings of anxiety and panic each time she thought about the impending interview. I told her to follow all the relaxation techniques that I describe in Chapter 8.

Step 3 – Don't Blush: I then tackled Rebecca's biggest worry – that she would turn red in the face when she opened her mouth to speak.

Blushing and embarrassment go hand in hand. We've all experienced those moments of self-consciousness that can trigger a reddening of the skin – most usually on the face. Blushing from embarrassment is connected to your 'fight-or-flight' response. As you find yourself in an awkward situation, your body automatically releases a rush of adrenaline that then causes your breathing and heart rate to speed up, enabling you to run away from this perceived danger, if you need to.

Adrenaline also causes your blood vessels to dilate in order to improve blood flow and oxygen delivery and this is the case with blushing. The veins in your face dilate and as more blood flows through them, your face becomes red. I explained to Rebecca that reducing her overall anxiety would help her to keep control over her adrenaline level.

I asked Rebecca to think back to the last time she blushed – could she remember what she was saying to herself? Usually people's internal dialogue goes something along the lines of, 'Oh no, I think I'm going to go red. Yes, I am, I just know it – I'm turning red. I hope they don't notice my face going red. I can feel it – it's starting to turn red. Great, last thing I wanted – my face going red!'

She agreed and realised exactly why her face did turn red. Her internal dialogue issued a command, her mind created a picture and her body followed – doing exactly as she had told it to.

I told her that she could easily take control of this by giving a different sort of command. The next time she felt herself starting to get that rush of adrenaline that signalled that her face might start turning red, all she simply needed to say was:

> 'I think I'm turning BLUE – yes, I am – I'm turning BLUE. I can feel that BLUENESS start to spread now across my face, my chest and down my arms even – I'm turning BLUE.'

As it's usual to feel heat rising up our faces, instruct this feeling to travel in a downwards direction:

> 'I can feel the BLUE start to drain down from the top of my head, down through my face, my eyes, my cheeks . . . down my neck, my shoulders, my chest. Yes, I'm definitely turning BLUE.'

Test this out – it works! And you can get some more ideas by downloading App 14.

Step 4 – The Future: We then worked together at generating some confidence and I created an anchor for her that she would be able to use before and during the interview – see App 10. We completed the session by creating a timeline – App 3 – and she was able to take a walk into the future, fully experiencing that upcoming interview with all that new-found confidence buzzing around inside her.

Case Study: The Exam Disaster Movie

When Ed came to see me, he was clearly a stressed young man. He told me he was having trouble sleeping, his skin had broken out in angry red rashes and his heart was racing.

He was facing his final exams at university and the anxiety of the whole process was starting to get to him. He had taken many exams in the past and had coped admirably, attaining very good grades. He was aware that positive thinking was the key to success – he'd witnessed many of his friends talk themselves into failure with their negativity – but this time the confidence he'd been able to summon up previously had simply evaporated. His entire academic career seemed to hinge on this one set of finals and his family was already looking forward to his graduation ceremony.

Ed had been working hard as usual, but this time his revision sessions seemed to be going badly. He found it difficult to concentrate or focus and at the end of each session he felt he simply hadn't done enough. He could already see that if he didn't change tack soon, the summer exams would end up being a disaster.

I told Ed that whilst there's no substitute for real knowledge acquired throughout the academic year, at this stage of the game it's the little things that count – the difference that makes all the difference. Just as you wouldn't dream of running a marathon without adequate training and preparation, it's best to enter this final phase of exams with a plan in mind.

If you have a look at the words that Ed used to describe his problem to me, you'll notice that he said he 'could already see disaster up ahead'. He had fallen into that well-known trap of creating a disaster movie for himself, with him taking the starring role of the guy who suffers a complete meltdown. What follows is an episode of blame, shame, embarrassment and recriminations. No wonder he was finding it difficult to revise!

Step 1 – Junking the Bad Stuff: I showed Ed how the bad pictures he was creating in his mind were running the show. He was able to get rid of them by downloading App 2 and then deal with those feelings of anxiety with App 25.

As well as working through the relaxation techniques in Chapter 5, I gave him a few extra tips to help him start having those revision sessions going the way he'd like them to:

1. **Keep your H.A.T. on:** If you are Hungry, Angry or Tired, your revision will not go well. Put these things right first and notice the difference.

2. **Eat well:** It's true what they say – 'junk food, junk mind'. If you want your body to be working at its best, you need to think about the fuel you put into it. Just like top footballers and athletes, you'll need some extra-special energy at this time. Avoid toxins such as excess sugar, alcohol and caffeine. Eat protein-rich food such as fish, turkey and chicken, and plenty of fruits and vegetables.

3. **Feeling grumpy or fed up of revision?:** Shake it out! Improving your circulation and the energy flow around your body makes it harder for you to hang on to negative feelings. Take regular exercise breaks such as a walk around the block. A couple of sessions of aerobic activity such as cycling, swimming or playing football each week will also improve those exam results.

4. **Avoid lie-ins:** Don't allow yourself to slip into 'holiday mode' during study leave – it will be that much harder to get up for an exam. This is especially important if your exam is in the afternoon – make sure you get up at your usual morning waking time and don't be tempted to have a lie-in.

5. **Location, location, location:** Choose your revision surroundings carefully, as the more these can match your exam room environment, the better. Lying on your bed or sitting in the garden under a tree may seem like a nice idea to make those hours of studying easier, but doing your revision at a table will get your body to associate this position with your studies. Recalling the information in exam conditions will be a lot easier when you adopt a similar pose.

6. **Give yourself space:** Try to position your desk or table away from the wall and have it face into the room or out of the

window. It's a lot easier to access information from the brain if there is a depth to your field of vision. If this is not possible, look up at the ceiling if you're struggling to remember something – the answer will come to you more easily as you point your eyes upwards. Remember, we see information in our minds as pictures and you need to have the space in front of you to be able to do this.

7. **Mind your language:** Keep a check on your internal dialogue. If you're hearing a constant stream of negative suggestions such as – 'What if I fail? I'm worried I might panic; I've forgotten everything!' – get rid of them by writing them all down on a piece of paper then screwing it up and throwing it away. Then you'll be able to insert a good dialogue – 'I will be calm and relaxed in the exam room; I will pass my exams with ease.'

8. **Blow away panic:** There's an easy solution if you start to feel those panicky feelings well up just as you enter the exam room. Imagine you're blowing up a balloon and blow out slowly for as long as you can. Repeat this three times. Those feelings of panic are created by the chemicals in your body and doing this exercise will enable you to blow them out.

9. **Track your progress:** It's very easy to look back on a day's revision and see all the things that went wrong, even if the reality is slightly different. Get a notebook and, each evening, write down three things that went really well with your revision. This will train your mind to focus on the positive aspects rather than getting locked into focusing on the negative ones. From now on, you'll easily get into the habit of thinking positively.

Step 2 – The Exam Success Movie: The second stage of our work together was to create a replacement for the 'disaster movie' we had eliminated. This is an important step, for too often people focus on getting rid of their bad feelings, then forget to insert some new feelings into the 'empty space'. Our minds find the absence of feelings very strange and so they'll automatically try to recover the old feelings rather than feel nothing at all. This is a common problem for people suffering from depression or phobias – they can successfully rid themselves of their bad feelings, only to have them bounce back shortly after. Getting your body to fill up with good feelings is the key to ensuring the bad feelings stay away.

Before we moved on to creating a new movie, I guided Ed through some of the apps: he downloaded App 10, Your Confidence Anchor; App 11, Supersize Your Confidence; and App 12, Circle of Excellence. With Ed feeling pumped up and full of confidence we were ready to work on the next stage.

If you'd like to do the same, follow these instructions. You may find it easier to get a friend to read the steps out loud to you – take your time and keep it slow.

1. Close your eyes and just imagine that you are watching a movie in your mind of your exam success story. It is a hot day and you are about to leave home to collect your exam results.
2. See yourself travelling to the centre and notice all the details. Are you alone in this image or with someone else? Notice the

colours, the sounds and even the clothes you're wearing. Fill in as many details as you can.

3. Imagine you have a remote control in your hand and turn the colours up brighter, bolder and stronger, and make the volume even louder. You can even add your own soundtrack to this movie – your favourite piece of music, which will act as your 'success theme'.

4. Now see yourself receiving your exam results in the way that you will – perhaps you'll be handed a brown envelope or maybe you'll need to search for your name on a list that's posted on the wall. See what you see and hear what you hear.

5. Continue running that movie forward and see the grades you've wanted so very badly. Really enjoy looking at these grades – these perfect grades!

6. As you see yourself in this movie, notice the expression on your face – the smile that tells you all is well. Make this picture a bit bigger and bring it even closer to you, turning up all the colours and the volume once more as you do so. Enjoy it! This is your special moment and it can be yours.

7. Now imagine floating up out of your chair and floating down into your body in this movie. Become the 'you' who's just received those brilliant results and jump up and down with excitement.

8. And when you've finished, you can simply open your eyes and come back into the room.

Practise this each day and by the time your exams come round, you will have set your mind and body onto that path of success.

And if your mind conjured up a theme tune for that movie of yours, why not play it to yourself on a daily basis? Remember, creating pictures like this in your mind will act as a magnet for your desired outcome, rather than simply being a case of wishful thinking. Good luck!

Case Study: My Big Fat Indian Wedding

Samir, thirty-two, came to see me and told me he was getting married. Although his future bride was the love of his life and he was delighted with how things had turned out, the wedding plans seemed to be spiralling out of control. He hadn't realised quite what would be involved.

It had escalated to four days of celebration with numerous relatives flying in from India and a banquet dinner arranged in a large London hotel. His future mother-in-law was quite a demanding lady who wanted to put on the best possible event.

Samir was worried, very worried. He just could not imagine himself getting up to make a speech in front of 300 guests at such a lavish venue. 'After all,' he told me, 'I'm just a quiet accountant – people in my profession don't tend to be loud and outgoing. I've never done anything like this before and I'm petrified. Plus, I just know my future wife's family are eager to check me out to see if I'm good enough for her.'

Fear of Public Speaking: As I told Samir, the fear of public speaking is the absolute number one fear and 75 per cent of us are said to suffer anxiety at the thought of getting up and speaking aloud in front of others. That's hundreds of millions of people around the world – so if this happens to be a fear of yours, you're in good company. Some surveys even show that people are less fearful of death.

It's commonly thought that this is something picked up from schooldays – so many of us were forced to read aloud to the class as our fellow pupils (and even teachers) sniggered and enjoyed watching every minute of our discomfort, so it's hardly surprising.

Some psychologists point out that as human beings, we have a built-in need to be accepted by our peers – it's important for our survival. Putting ourselves forward in order to be judged means we potentially jeopardise this – hence the feelings of anxiety.

Whilst a place on the stage may be easy to avoid if the limelight is not quite your cup of tea, there are all too many work or social occasions when it's harder to avoid. There's little doubt that being fearful of speaking aloud has negative effects on so many careers, limiting the success we can achieve.

Whether you're planning to give an important speech or business presentation, perform on stage or audition for *The X Factor*(!), this section will teach you how to control those feelings of anxiety.

I began by telling Samir about a well-known interview with Bruce Springsteen. When asked if he ever felt nervous about performing on stage, he emphatically replied, 'Never.' The interviewer was surprised to hear this as most performers he'd interviewed had confessed to some feelings of anxiety.

So he questioned 'The Boss' further, asking him if he could really not remember noticing any feelings of nervousness at all.

Bruce Springsteen replied, 'No, never at all. Just before I go on stage my heart begins to beat a little faster . . . my hands start to sweat a little . . . my legs start to feel numb, as if I'm getting pins and needles . . . and then I get a tight feeling in the pit of my stomach that begins to spin round and round . . . When I get all of those feelings, I know I'm excited, pumped up and ready to go on stage.'

Now I don't know about you, but most people experiencing those kinds of feelings would describe them as extreme nervousness and anxiety! What Bruce cleverly did was re-label those feelings as something different and associate them with having a good time on stage. As far as he was concerned, he was experiencing feelings of excitement – and how we respond to the feelings inside our body has a profound effect on our behaviour.

Step 1 – Change Your Mind Pictures: I asked Samir to think about the pictures that came into his mind each time he thought about giving that speech. He hadn't realised he was making pictures, but could instantly recognise that his mother-in-law's face was looming large in front of him, with a great big scowl on her face.

I gave him instructions on how to get rid of this – move the picture further away, drain the colours out and start shrinking it down till it's nothing more than a dot. Take your imaginary paintbrush and whiten it all out. See the full details in App 2.

Then I suggested that we put good pictures in place of those old ones. I asked him what would be most helpful to him. He chose a picture of his beautiful bride-to-be. Very appropriate, I told him. He called her image up in front of him and I instructed him to turn the colours up bright and bold and to make that picture much larger and bring it closer to him – App 1.

He did this and could immediately see the sense of it as it made him feel much better.

Step 2 – Change the Voices: Having tackled the pictures, I then asked Samir if he was hearing any voices – what was his internal dialogue saying to him as he thought about the wedding. He listened carefully and realised he could hear his own voice repeatedly saying, 'You're going to look a fool, you're going to look a fool.' I asked him if he could change the sound of that voice so it resembled Mickey Mouse, Donald Duck or any other character that came to his mind. He did this and had to admit that it sounded ridiculous. In fact, it made him laugh. This was good news, as laughter is a great way of changing your emotional state – it's pretty hard to feel anxious and laugh at the same time.

He created an imaginary volume control, and then I asked him to turn the volume right the way down on that voice. With the voice of doom now gone, he felt much better.

I asked him to seek out a 'success theme tune' for himself. To find a piece of music that made him feel pumped up and ready to go each time he heard it – perhaps the current favourite on his iPod or the uplifting theme tune from a movie. Anything that felt right for him. I told him to play it to himself regularly over the next few days as he practised the NLP techniques I was going to show him. Next time he thought about the wedding his 'success theme tune' would be what he'd hear, rather than those voices.

Step 3 – Lose that Anxiety: I began tackling Samir's feelings of anxiety. He told me that every time he thought about the speech, he'd feel a grinding, sick feeling in the pit of his stomach. I explained to him that it's possible to reverse those feelings and used App 25.

This is a good technique as he'd be able to use it throughout the day as and, when he needed to, especially when he stood up to give that speech.

Step 4 – A New You: The next step was to transform Samir from that shy, retiring accountant into an outgoing personality. App 9 – Creating a New You – enabled him to rehearse his new voice and his new posture. Once he had a clear idea of how he would like to come across at the reception, he rehearsed his speech using this new-found demeanour.

Step 5 – The Future: I then asked Samir to practise his performance at home while looking in the mirror. Having the opportunity to really let himself go in the privacy of his own home allowed him to make refinements.

I told him it was possible to imagine transporting the mirror he'd been rehearsing in front of to his reception. As he stood up to give his speech on the wedding day itself he'd be able to place his imaginary portable mirror in front of him – App 13. He felt safe at the thought of having this imaginary barrier between himself and the audience.

Samir came to see me for a total of three sessions and we were able to play around with all the skills that I had taught him. He downloaded a Confidence Anchor, App 10, and practised his performance using the Circle of Excellence, App 12.

We finished off by eliciting his timeline – App 3 – and I had him walk into his future. On his timeline he was able to experience the upcoming event, and, most importantly, he was able to walk along his line to just *after* the event had taken place. He was able to experience seeing himself being congratulated for giving a good speech, surrounded by a sea of smiling relatives.

And just as a bonus, I stretched Samir's timeline a little more so he could take a few steps further – into his honeymoon! As soon as he did this, his body relaxed a little more and a big smile came over his face so I asked him to anchor those good feelings too – App 10.

When Samir thought about giving that wedding speech now, he could see it as a means to an end – and a particularly good one at that!

12

Fix Your Fears and Phobias

Too often the reason why we fail to fulfil our potential and become truly successful is, quite simply, fear. Imagine being able to wipe out feelings of fear in just a few minutes – how good would you feel? Close your eyes for a few moments and just imagine a life without feelings of fear and anxiety. Where would you go? Who would you meet? What would you do if you knew you could not possibly fail?

Some of you will imagine yourselves sky-diving or performing some other equally daredevil activity. Others will see themselves simply catching an aeroplane and taking a holiday abroad. I wonder how you're seeing yourself? Perhaps you've plucked up the courage to ask your boss for a pay rise? Or ask someone out on a date?

Ironically, most of the things that we worry about never happen, so we hold ourselves back for nothing. Feelings of fear and anxiety are just that – feelings – and the good thing about feelings is that they can be changed. The trick is knowing how to do it.

Fears, Phobias, Anxiety – What's the Difference?

Fear is a natural and essential human emotion: being programmed with the ability to have feelings of fear is what saved our ancestors from being eaten by sabre-toothed tigers. In fact, the ones that felt too little fear were the ones who got eaten and eventually died out! Today, that sudden rush of adrenaline is what enables you to jump out of the way of an oncoming vehicle.

That said, human beings are actually born with only two types of fear – a fear of loud noises and the fear of falling. Every other fear known to mankind has been downloaded along the way, either with the help of your parents or teachers (who taught you useful things such as touching a naked flame will burn you) or through your own experiences and or seeing those of others.

It's understandable, then, for people to believe that phobias can run in families or that a gene for shyness really does exist. But whilst some of us may have a propensity to be less or more anxious, our subsequent programming can take the blame for everything else.

Phobias do not simply involve intense fear, they can seem completely irrational, quite random and persist over a long period of time. I've come across people who have phobias of buttons, zips, tomatoes and pens that 'click' at the top. As long as they are able to avoid the object of their fears, people feel fine, but whereas it may be possible to avoid stepping onto an aeroplane, for example, it's very much harder to avoid ordinary day-to-day objects. The feelings of panic then begin to build up as the stress of avoidance becomes too much to bear. The phobia becomes distorted as the fear is really related to a fear of panic, rather than the object itself.

In these cases, the phobia has been created by an underlying feeling of anxiety that went unchecked for many years. Dealing with this in the first instance will go a long way to diminishing the phobia's power. Learning relaxation techniques, taking more exercise and making adjustments to your diet, such as avoiding the yo-yo effects of excess sugar, may be all that's required – read through the reducing anxiety tips I give below.

Other phobias can develop as a result of a bad experience – being bitten by a dog or flying in a plane that's hit by lightning, for example, will create a natural desire to avoid a similar encounter. For these types of fears, NLP techniques used quickly after the event can enable you to avoid years of misery. In fact, as the phobia can be downloaded in seconds, it makes sense to rid yourself of it in a similar amount of time. Taking several months to talk through the bad event with a psychotherapist can sometimes make the phobia seem 'more real' and as it becomes more deeply imprinted on your mind, it's that much harder to dispel.

Top Tips for Reducing Anxiety

1. **Diet**: Be aware that certain foods can alter our stress and anxiety levels as well as create mood swings. A complex-carbohydrate-rich, low-glycaemic-index diet can reduce

anxiety, raise serotonin levels and aid restful sleep. Foods to eat plenty of include: porridge, boiled potatoes, brown rice, wholegrain breads, fish, turkey, chicken, cottage cheese, avocados, beans, less ripe bananas, plenty of fruit and vegetables in general.

2. **Avoid toxins**: Be aware that these too will interfere with our feelings and create mood swings. Reduce caffeine levels – e.g. coffee, tea, chocolate, coffee-flavoured ice-cream and cakes. Be aware of the stimulating effects of cheese, red meat, alcohol and nicotine. It's also wise to reduce salt intake.

3. **Vitamins and minerals:** Refined and processed foods make it harder for our body to do its work. When you suffer from fear or anxiety-related problems, your biochemical processes are knocked off-balance even further. To help your system cope better when you have an anxiety problem it's advisable to supplement your diet with the following vitamins and minerals, or seek help from a nutritionist:
   - **Vitamin B complex:** B vitamins help the nervous system function properly; a deficiency of these vitamins can sometimes produce mental changes, e.g. anxiety, irritability, fatigue, emotional instability.
   - **Vitamin C:** This helps the adrenal glands to function properly. This is important as these glands have to work so much harder when you are anxious or under stress.

- **Calcium and magnesium:** These have a soothing effect on the nervous system; they are natural tranquillisers. If you lack calcium, you will feel nervous and on edge very easily. Calcium and magnesium are best taken together as they enhance each other's absorption into the body.
- **Zinc:** This has an influence on growth and on resistance to infection. It is also involved in normal hormone production and normal mental function. It has a stabilising effect on the nervous system and is nowadays prescribed to counter-balance anxiety.

4. **Exercise:** When we experience stress, anxiety or fear on a regular basis, we get into a state of continual emotional upheaval, and that leads to an inability to relax physically. It's usual for muscles to tense up, for us to sweat, have an increased pulse rate as the heart begins to race, jaw muscles to clench, hands get tingly, to name just a few symptoms. The higher our physical tension levels, the more likely it is that we will experience further bouts of anxiety. Regular exercise (at least twenty minutes each day), such as walking, uses up excess adrenaline and releases endorphins, thereby reducing stress levels. Ideally take brisk exercise in the late afternoon.

5. **Goals:** We often begin to feel anxious when we forget or lose sight of our goals. Make a list of all the things you want to achieve to remind yourself. Spend a few moments visualising that future – make the picture bigger, brighter,

bolder and stronger. Then make a list of all your good qualities – reasons why you know you will achieve those goals. Praise yourself generously.

6. **Visualisation:** Spend as much time as possible imagining success. Whatever you spend a lot of time visualising will eventually come true, and that goes for positive and negative images! Imagining negative things makes a negative outcome more likely. Expecting successful outcomes makes success more likely. Expect problems and you jeopardise your outcome.

Eliminating Anxiety in the Waiting Room

Dr Popat, a dentist, contacted me and asked me to give him some tips for helping his patients to feel more relaxed. Quite often the five-minute-or-so wait in the waiting room before the appointment would be the point at which their anxiety would start to rise.

When a sense of fear develops inside the body it's being triggered by a build-up of anxiety chemicals such as cortisol. One of the quickest ways to rid yourself of these is to breathe *out* deeply and literally blow them away. It's quite common for people in stressful situations to remind themselves to 'take a deep breath', but in fact anxiety often builds up because too much air has collected inside our lungs due to the tension inside our bodies. This results in a tightness in the chest and the panicky feeling of not being able to breathe. As we try to take another deep breath in, we discover that we can't easily do it and so start to feel even more anxious. Imagine that you are blowing up a balloon and blow out slowly and deeply three or four times instead – this will make all the difference.

Any Monsters or Dragons?: Too often, those last few minutes in the waiting room are accompanied by our over-imaginative thoughts, which as we've discovered are made up of pictures and internal dialogue. The quickest way to change your feelings is to change these images:

1. Become aware of the worrying thought that you are having and of the pictures and sounds that accompany that thought.

2. Imagine holding a remote control in your hand and turn the colour down on those pictures, making them less bright.

3. And if there's any internal dialogue that goes with that picture, turn the volume right down.

4. Continue adjusting the picture – drain all the colour out of it and start shrinking it right down till it's nothing more than a dot . . . and send it far away.

Once you have cleared your mind, you can bring yourself back to the present moment and focus on your surroundings. After all, those natural feelings of anxiety were handed down to you by your ancestors to protect you from monsters and dragons. If you are perfectly safe in the 'here and now', you have no need to feel anxious. We don't know what will be happening to you later on in the day, but what we do know is that at this precise moment you are safe and well. Keep asking yourself – any monsters or dragons? If the answer is 'no', you can relax.

Your Secret Hideaway: Finally, you can take shelter in 'Your Secret Hideaway' – App 29. Here you'll be able to create a special place where you can always feel relaxed – remember, it's the pictures in your mind that are running the show. It's common to hear suggestions that you imagine a nice, sunny beach but I'm going to recommend that you take a little more time to think about this. Where would you really feel at your most safe and relaxed? It could be indoors rather than outdoors. One of my clients felt at her safest when she was riding a horse. And who would you be with? It could be someone you know, someone you've yet to meet, or your hero from a movie. It's your secret hideaway so it can look any way you'd like it to look. Enjoy!

Case Study: Erasing Bad Memories

Jean, sixty, had recently been involved in a car accident. As she crossed a busy junction another car shot straight out and hit her car in the side. Fortunately no one was seriously hurt and the cars were easily repaired over the next few weeks. Although shaken up initially, Jean felt she'd dealt with the situation and it was over and done with. However, a month later she started having trouble sleeping and as she lay awake at night her mind would begin to race. It was during these episodes in the middle of the night that her thoughts would return to the accident. Everyone had emerged safely, but in her imagination Jean started to relive those events with a far unhappier ending. She could hear the screeching of the tyres and even smell the burning rubber. Her heart would pound and she was beginning to feel exhausted after all these sleepness nights. She was fearful of even going to bed at night now, as she just knew the nightmares would return.

Step 1 – Control Anxiety: I explained to Jean that as she conjured up the images of the accident in her mind, her body responded by releasing adrenaline and cortisol which create the pounding heart and feelings of anxiety. In turn, her mind registered the feelings of anxiety and, believing that there must be something to panic about, created more scary pictures. And so on.

In order to break this cycle, I showed Jean how to do a number of breathing and relaxation exercises as detailed in Chapter 8. It was going to be important for her to be able to control these feelings in the middle of the night. I also encouraged her to create a 'Secret Hideaway' for herself – App 29.

Step 2 – Lose Those Memories: I worked with Jean on erasing those bad memories of the accident. The NLP Fast Phobia Cure – App 26 – is now an established technique for getting rid of these kinds of thoughts.

1. I asked Jean to relax and close her eyes. And then to bring back to her mind the memory that was continuing to plague her at night. The bad car accident that she had been involved in recently.

2. I asked her to remember the moment just before the accident – the point at which she was completely safe and to remember, too, that she was completely safe after the accident.

3. Then I asked her to imagine herself sitting in a cinema in the front row, watching herself on a small black and white screen, in a movie of the events as they took place.

4. Then I asked Jean to imagine getting out of her seat and walking to the back of the cinema and up into the projection booth.

5. Once she was here I told her she could look down onto the screen in safety and watch that movie.

6. I told her that the movie is going to start *before* the bad experience and end *after* it's over and she is safe.

7. Once it had reached the end, I asked her to freeze it into a still picture.

8. Then to imagin that she floats up into the picture on the screen and becomes the 'Jean' in that image.

9. I asked her to change the picture into colour and allow the events to run backwards as she took part in them.

10. This starts at the end of the episode and rewinds back quickly to the beginning of the episode – before the bad experience ever occurred.

11. I asked her to do this quickly, so it takes a few seconds only.

12. Then to repeat it again, running this movie with her inside it, from the very end all the way back to the very beginning.

13. To add a little circus-style music to accompany these ridiculous events – with people walking backwards and talking backwards. Everything running backwards.

14. I asked Jean to repeat this again – from the end all the way back to the beginning.

15. I then asked her to end the movie with her, in complete safety, looking and feeling calm and happy – before the event ever happened.

I then asked Jean to open her eyes when she felt ready to do so. When she thought back to the experience, she was able to call to mind the accident, but couldn't bring back the same feelings of anxiety that she had been experiencing before. This procedure can be repeated if the person feels it needs reinforcing.

Step 3 – Add Good Feelings: I then reminded Jean about the importance of adding in some good feelings. It's not uncommon for people to feel as if they have an empty space in their minds once they've got rid of their bad memories or feelings. In these instances, the mind can be eager to hang on to the bad thoughts in order to fill the gap – anything is preferable to that feeling of emptiness.

Whilst Jean was back on the road driving her car, she still found herself avoiding the street where the accident happened. So I created a relaxing trance state for her and enabled her to visualise herself driving along that same stretch of road, but this time with good, confident feelings – App 10.

Case Study: Fear of Flying

Daniel, thirty-two, had built up a fear of flying over many years. His childhood holidays had all been taken in England, so he'd never had the opportunity to fly at a young age. His first flight abroad had been on a 'lads' weekend' to Barcelona in his early twenties. Needless to say, the weekend had been a raucous one that had resulted in several of his mates getting very drunk.

The flight to Spain hadn't been too bad, and while Daniel had felt nervous, it had been uneventful. Coming back, though, it was a different story. Two of his friends were still pretty drunk and wouldn't stop fooling around. They picked up on Daniel's nervousness and started to tease him, filling his head with horror stories about plane crashes. On board the aeroplane, the stewardess had issued them with warnings about their behaviour and even threatened them with arrest at their destination. As Daniel was sitting next to his mates, he spent most of the flight trying to control their behaviour, which added to his feelings of anxiety. Once they were back in the UK, Daniel vowed he would never fly again until he had successfully 'anchored' feelings of anxiety to the thought of flying in an aeroplane.

Since that time, Daniel had in fact plucked up the courage and flown abroad another couple of times. Each time, though, he had been highly nervous during the week before travel, with sleepless nights and an upset stomach. The journey itself was pretty painful and he often sat on the plane shaking.

Whilst Daniel had just about managed to do the travelling he wanted to, things had now changed. He was due to get married in a couple of months' time and a honeymoon in America had been arranged. Whilst his fiancée was aware of his anxieties, he had played them down in the past. Now, he did not want his fear of flying to ruin the honeymoon.

Step 1 – Dealing with Anxiety: Daniel had no strong memories of the fateful flight he'd experienced on that lads' weekend. It had been several years ago and he could now look back and almost laugh about it, but for some reason the feelings still stayed with him.

For this reason, I did not feel it was appropriate to use the NLP Fast Phobia Cure, which works best when someone has a phobic response that contains flashbacks of the bad experience.

Daniel was experiencing anxiety attacks and a straightforward fear of flying in the future, rather than specifically remembering something that happened in the past.

I showed Daniel how to deal with his feelings of anxiety by teaching him the relaxation techniques detailed in Chapter 8. I encouraged him to use these on a daily basis before his trip both during the day and at night if he had trouble sleeping.

In addition, I showed him a self-hypnosis technique, which I adapted to suit his plane journey. I taught Daniel the following phrases:

'Now I'm aware that I can see . . .'
'Now I'm aware that I can hear . . .'
'Now I'm aware that I can feel . . .'

As we worked together, I asked Daniel to say out loud each sentence three times. In the gap, I asked him to put an appropriate word (i.e. whatever it was he was seeing, hearing or feeling).

During the session, he inserted the words 'window, light fitting and books' for things that he could see. Then 'clock ticking, traffic in the street and sound of my breathing' for things that he could hear. He then went on to use the words 'cushion behind my back, floor beneath my feet and chair that I'm sitting on' for things that he could feel.

The object of this exercise is to take your attention, awareness and focus away from the bigger picture of what is happening around you, enabling you to simply focus on the things immediately around you. You shrink your world and notice only what is around you.

During a flight, Daniel would be able to slot different words into the gaps – e.g. 'the seat pocket in front of me, the in-flight magazine, the checked fabric of the seat in front of me' for things that he could see.

It's possible to take this technique one step further by closing your eyes and describing what you see in your imagination rather than what you actually see. So it could be a nice, sunny beach, a field or a meadow.

Step 2 – Reversing Anxiety: With Daniel having several relaxation techniques under his belt for use during the flight we now concentrated on his other big fear – the check-in queue. He usually managed to get himself to the airport in a fairly upbeat mood, but once he joined that queue (which always moved so slowly) the panic would start to set in. Here was his last opportunity to turn back and run. Once checked in, he felt locked into the system.

As Daniel stood in that queue, he could feel the anxiety inside his stomach. It felt as if it were moving around and almost made him feel sick. I explained that in order for him to keep on feeling those feelings, they have to be moving. If they were static, he simply wouldn't be able to feel them any more. I showed Daniel how he could take control and get them to move in the opposite direction and so bring about a halt to the sensation.

Once the feelings were moving in a different direction, Daniel felt much better. Increasing the spinning sensation actually enabled him to trigger some good feelings. You can do the same by downloading App 25.

Step 3 – Confident Anchor: Daniel practised creating a 'Confident Anchor' – App 10 – many times over, ensuring that it felt really powerful for when he needed it most. He used it in the check-in queue and also as he was boarding the flight.

Step 4 – The Future: The last stage of our work together was to get Daniel to 'mentally rehearse' his future – visualising himself taking that plane journey while having calm feelings inside him.

I guided him into a hypnotic trance and whilst he was feeling deeply relaxed, I took him on a journey that began with him leaving home in the morning. With his suitcase packed and his fiancée by his side, he could see himself climbing into a taxi and heading off for the airport. I had him arrive at the airport and see himself paying the taxi driver, wheeling his suitcase into the departure lounge, finding the correct queue, joining it and checking himself in. He watched his boarding pass being printed and his passport being checked.

All throughout this session, I invited him to fully 'associate' into the scene, so that rather than looking at himself, he had actually 'become' himself – he could see through his eyes everything as it happened. The hypnosis ended after he had completed the flight, feeling happy and calm, and had landed at his destination.

This is a very clever way of tricking the body into believing that it has already done something 'for real'. Daniel came to see me for three sessions, so by the time he really did take that journey, he truly believed flying was the one of the most relaxing ways to travel.

13

Fix Your Health and Wellbeing

How the mind influences the body's immune system has been a source of fascination since the beginning of modern medicine, with books published on the subject as early as 1915. The term psycho-neuro-immunology was more recently coined in 1975 by the scientists Robert Ader and Nicholas Cohen as a result of their work based on the original 'conditioned-reponse' experiments carried out by Pavlov with his dogs, as detailed in Chapter 5. Since that time, the study of the relationship between mental processes and health has been one of the fastest-growing fields in modern science.

Research has shown that the brain and immune system 'talk' to each other all the time, and improving this communication can be instrumental in maintaining good health. In addition, hypnosis and NLP are very effective at altering pain perception and suppressing the secretion of stress hormones.

Overcoming Stress

It can be easy to get locked into a cycle of stress, as events and situations in our day-to-day lives create stressful thoughts which in turn trigger a range of responses in our bodies, from physical complaints such as skin problems, insomnia, irritable bowel syndrome and asthma to emotional problems such as tearfulness or anger and behavioural problems such as forgetfulness.

These type of symptoms then trigger yet more stressful thoughts and the cycle continues.

Breaking this cycle can prove difficult for some people, as feeling stressed can quickly become a habit. NLP can help you to gain control over your nervous system and become aware of the thought processes that affect your physiology, emotions and behaviour.

Your Early Warning System: Most of us can tell when we feel stressed – but usually by the time we feel the effects, our bodies have been negatively affected for some time. Once the effects become deeply entrenched, it can become very much harder to get ourselves back on track. Creating an 'early warning system' will enable you to recognise when it's time to take action.

Read the following list of symptoms and mark the ones which you tend to experience most when you are under stress. Select three of the most common symptoms from each category – these can then be used as your own 'early warning system'.

Symptoms
Physical
- ☐ rapid shallow breathing and palpitations
- ☐ tight chest
- ☐ indigestion
- ☐ stomach cramps
- ☐ shoulder, neck and back pain
- ☐ persistent headaches
- ☐ chronic sinus problems
- ☐ humming in the ears
- ☐ frequent viral infections
- ☐ weight loss or gain
- ☐ frequent urination
- ☐ constipation or diarrhoea
- ☐ skin problems
- ☐ tired eyes and visual disturbances
- ☐ stiffness
- ☐ frequent 'pins and needles'
- ☐ attacks of dizziness

Emotional
- ☐ an increase in anxiety and fearfulness
- ☐ becoming easily hurt and upset
- ☐ being tearful
- ☐ feeling irritable
- ☐ having a sense of worthlessness and apathy
- ☐ lacking confidence
- ☐ being confused or overwhelmed
- ☐ being humourless
- ☐ getting over-excited

Behavioural

- [ ] poor concentration, an inability to listen well
- [ ] forgetfulness
- [ ] over-activity, restlessness, talking too much
- [ ] nervous habits such as biting nails
- [ ] inability to make decisions and sort priorities
- [ ] poor planning, reluctance to delegate
- [ ] 'making mountains out of molehills'
- [ ] an increase in phobic fears and obsessions
- [ ] increased consumption of alcohol, nicotine, etc.
- [ ] insomnia and nightmares
- [ ] impotence and loss of libido
- [ ] unkempt appearance and untidiness
- [ ] loss of control over finances
- [ ] over-protectiveness and over-cautiousness

Please note that you should be able to spot the physical and emotional signs yourself, but you may not be so aware of the behavioural ones, so you may need to ask someone else, such as a close friend or colleague, to help you monitor these.

Make a promise to yourself that if you or anyone else notices that you have the following symptoms, you will take steps to de-stress yourself and take extra care:

Body	Emotions	Behaviour
....	....	....
....	....	....
....	....	....

Remember This

If after following all the techniques, you still find yourself with unexplained symptoms, a visit to the doctor for a check-up is advisable.

Once you have your 'early warning system' in place, you'll then need to decide what steps you're going to take to de-stress yourself. You'll find the relaxation techniques detailed in Chapter 8 particularly helpful and the most appropriate apps to download are 24, 25 and 27.

In addition, my advice to my clients is to consider stimulating those senses that they use less. For example, if you sit in front of a computer screen all day at work, I wouldn't recommend a trip to the cinema for relaxation. Walking outside in the fresh air or listening to music would be a better bet.

Burning aromatherapy candles and exciting your taste buds with different types of foods will also 'light up' the parts of your brain that your work wouldn't normally reach.

And remember, relaxation can be energetic. Have you ever turned up for work on a Monday morning after a really energetic weekend away with friends feeling far more relaxed than if you'd spent a quiet weekend mooching around the house?

Not only do our bodies need to relax – but our minds do too. Anything that breaks your normal pattern of thinking and gets your brain working in a different way is going to feel relaxing.

Case Study: Stress in the City

A City high-flyer, Laurel, thirty-four, could not be more proud of the successful career she had carved out for herself. Her adrenaline-fuelled days were usually rounded off with several rounds of drinks in the local wine bar with her work colleagues – she worked hard and played hard. However, she was beginning to realise that her lifestyle was beginning to take its toll and that she would have to start changing her habits in order to continue operating at such a high level.

Avoiding the after-work drinks and establishing a routine of early nights seemed like a good idea, but Laurel found that if she went home early without letting off steam, her mind would continue to 'buzz' till the early hours of the morning. Even worse, she'd developed the symptoms of IBS – she could no longer relax and focus on her work as she never knew when she'd need to rush off to the loo. She knew she should take steps to feel more relaxed, but didn't know where to begin.

Step 1 – Peace and Calm: I began by showing Laurel how easy it could be to trigger a sensation of peace and calm in the body and helped her to download App 27 – Your Calm Anchor.

1. Once she was sitting comfortably, I invited her to close her eyes and allow her body to gently begin relaxing and to become aware of her breathing.
2. I asked her to remember a moment in the past when she felt completely relaxed and stress-free – perhaps relaxing in a nice warm bath, or lying on a sunny beach. Or perhaps

a stress-free moment that was more active such as cycling outdoors with the wind blowing through her hair or even horseriding. A moment that made her feel happy, content and relaxed. I told her to enjoy the feelings that this image brings up.

3. I asked her to make the image more vivid by making the colours brighter, bolder and stronger. And then to make the sounds louder and the picture bigger.

4. Laurel continued to make that picture bigger and bring it closer – really enjoying this moment of relaxation and making those feelings stronger.

5. As those calming, relaxing feelings began to grow and reach a peak, I asked her to *squeeze her middle finger and thumb* on her dominant hand tightly together, capturing all the good feelings there. She held them closed for a few moments.

6. I then asked her to open her hand and we repeated this process three more times, ensuring she took the time to really enjoy each experience.

Each time she squeezed her fingers while feeling those calm, relaxed feelings she was creating a 'calming anchor' for herself. If ever in the future Laurel finds herself feeling stressed about a particular situation, event or person, all she has to do is squeeze her fingers together in the same way and these good, calm feelings will automatically flood her body.

Combining this anchor with some of the other relaxation techniques detailed in Chapter 8 will make this technique even more powerful.

Step 2 – Laugh Out Loud: Laurel also told me that she couldn't remember the last time she'd found anything remotely funny or laughed out loud. The long working hours had meant losing touch with friends, and hobbies were a distant memory.

Laughing in response to day-to-day problems may not be an obvious choice for most of us, but experts are agreed that it may be the best medicine.

Laughter is one of the body's in-built healing mechanisms that help us to cope with life. That's why so many of us can find ourselves accidentally laughing at funerals – our bodies are automatically aiding our recovery.

Hanging on to bad emotions for too long can have damaging effects on our bodies. Laughing out loud will not only trigger a release of endorphins – the body's natural painkillers that produce a sense of wellbeing – but will also lower blood pressure and boost immune function. It can also help us to release other emotions such as anger and boredom. If you feel you need to create a more positive outlook, find a solution to a tricky problem, or just plain feel better, follow these tips:

1. Watch funny movies, TV programmes or listen to comedy on the radio.
2. Arrange a visit to a comedy club to see a live performance.
3. Have a laughter competition with your friends to see who can laugh loudest and longest.
4. Wear a light-hearted tie or scarf to work. Or funny underwear if you have to go to a serious meeting or usually wear a uniform.

5. If laughing out loud seems a step too far, try deliberately wearing a smile for the rest of the day and notice how good it makes you feel.

Step 3 – Calm the Stomach: Next, we talked about Laurel's IBS and how she could control the symptoms. As well as having her follow all the relaxation techniques in Chapter 8, I gave her a relaxation CD to listen to each evening when she came home from work.

She told me she still experienced problems during the day, usually just after lunch. I showed her how to download App 28, A Calm Stomach, and it became a routine. Each day she would take a few moments to close her eyes and follow the steps both before going out to lunch and on her return to the office. Follow these steps if you would like to do the same:

1. Take a minute to get comfortable, relax and breathe out deeply three times. *(Visualisation exercises are more powerful if you are relaxed, so this is an important point.)*
2. Focus down into your stomach area and imagine it becoming warmer and warmer. As it does, allow this warmth to penetrate the rest of your body.
3. Imagine making yourself very small – so small that you can get into your stomach and walk around inside it. *(You may find it easier to do this with your eyes closed.)*
4. Picture the inside of your stomach – perhaps it resembles a cave – and become aware of the moisture dripping off the walls. This is the excess acid that causes you problems.

5. See yourself walking around the inside of your stomach with a big, soft sponge. It's very absorbent and you can use it to gently mop up all the excess acid from the walls and the floor.

6. Keep wiping off all the moisture, until there is none left.

7. You can leave your stomach now. Imagine becoming your normal size again, focusing on the nice, clean feeling you have on the inside.

Case Study: A Good Night's Sleep

Stephen came to see me soon after he was made redundant, aged forty. Not surprisingly, he had a lot on his mind: how to continue with those mortgage payments and how to find a new job. He knew he should be keeping upbeat, confident and ready for interviews, but his worries seemed to envelop him at night-time and a good night's sleep was becoming a distant memory.

Most of us have experienced insomnia or difficulty sleeping at one time or another. It's estimated that 30 to 50 per cent of us are affected by insomnia and 10 per cent have chronic insomnia that can last for many years.

Various sleep problems, such as difficulty falling asleep or having a problem with maintaining sleep through the night and even a perception of a poor night's sleep, can all be classed as insomnia. It can be defined as an inadequate quantity or quality of sleep, rather than a specific number of hours that a person gets – for each of us has differing sleep requirements.

The most common causes of sleeping problems are alcohol, jet lag, changes in shift work, and stressful life situations such as exams, divorce, bereavement, unemployment or an illness. For many people, this proves to be a temporary problem that corrects itself automatically. For others, however, the effects are felt for much longer as their bodies quickly habituate to patterns of interrupted sleep and they struggle to regain their natural rhythm.

The daytime effects of insomnia include the following:

- Poor concentration and focus
- Difficulty with memory
- Poor motor co-ordination
- Irritability
- Increased car accidents because of fatigue

The majority of people suffering from insomnia fail to get help or treatment for their problem, and the reasons given for this are the desire to avoid sleeping pills which can cause a residual fuzziness the next day and also the possibility of a chemical dependence on them.

However, as you've already discovered throughout this book – problems that are created in the mind are best solved through the mind. To begin with, however, I gave Stephen my top tips for putting yourself back into a cycle of restful sleep.

Top Tips for a Good Night's Sleep:
1. Start getting up half an hour earlier each day. As difficult as this may sound, there are so many studies that have now been carried out to support this theory, with demonstrable

good results, that it would be foolish to ignore this advice. So if you usually set your alarm for 7 a.m. each morning, set it for 6.30 a.m. in future.

2. Stick to this routine throughout the weekends too. It's common to want to catch up on lost sleep at the weekends, but remember, you're trying to establish a new routine for yourself and this is going to be much harder to do if your Monday-to-Friday habits get thrown off balance by your weekend ones. You'll also discover the benefit of feeling better on that Monday morning.

3. From now on, don't go to bed unless you really feel as if you are ready to go to sleep. Too many of us head off to bed because we feel we ought to or because it's our usual time. But waiting an extra half-hour or so may make all the difference between getting into a deep sleep quickly or spending a couple of hours tossing and turning.

4. No matter how tired you feel during the day, never take a nap. All your sleeping time must now take place at night and only ever in your bed. Daytime naps encourage your body to get into the habit of sleeping for a short while, only to quickly wake up again – exactly the habit you're trying to get your body out of.

5. Check out your bedroom environment – is your bed truly comfortable? A quick way to check is to compare your bed to those you sleep in on holidays and in hotels. If they always feel less comfortable than the one you sleep in all the time, you'll know you've got it right. And what about your bedding? Would a new pillow or duvet help you to feel more

relaxed? Buy the best-quality linen you can afford for your bed – the higher the thread count in the sheets the softer they will feel.

6. Aim to sleep in a dark room – studies show that the darker the bedroom the deeper the sleep. And check the temperature of the room – it should be cool.

7. Clear your clutter – it's not unusual to find a whole array of electrical goods in modern bedrooms – TVs, computers, clock radios, mobile phones, iPods, etc. Leaving these on standby or charging by the side of the bed will fill your room with an invisible electrically charged atmosphere that will interfere with your sleep.

8. Avoid eating late at night – the earlier you can eat before bedtime the more relaxed your body will feel. Digesting large meals requires quite a lot of energy from your body – if possible leave as long as three hours between eating and sleeping.

9. Avoid toxins – caffeine, alcohol, nicotine, sugar – and beware the stimulating effects of red meat and cheese.

10. Have a pad of paper and a pen by the side of the bed – if you find a problem starts to niggle at night, you'll be able to write it down and forget it. You'll find your pen and paper handy, too, first thing in the morning – it's when the 'genius' part of our minds gives us good ideas.

Armed with his set of rules, Stephen could already see things that he could easily fix to help break that cycle. We then worked together for three sessions, during which he was able to practise relaxing – something he realised he hadn't been able to do properly for a very long time.

At the end of the process, he was familiar with all the relaxation techniques in Chapter 8 and we downloaded Apps 27, Your Calm Anchor, and 29, Your Secret Hideaway, for use at night-time.

Box Up Your Worries: I also taught him how to 'Box Up Your Worries' – App 24. Worries are those emotional messages that our minds send us because they're trying to look out for us – they have our best interests at heart. Acknowledging receipt of these messages is often all you need to do to make them go away, for you'll trick your mind into believing that you've taken action.

1. Find a box. It can be an old shoebox or a small attractively decorated one. Any sort that feels right for you. This is going to be your 'worry box'.
2. Each time you feel worried, get some paper and write down your worry.
3. Think about what might be making you feel like this and write this down too.
4. Once you have finished, fold the piece of paper up and put it into your box. Put the lid firmly on the box and put it away.
5. By writing down your worry, you will have sent an important message to your unconscious mind – letting it know that you have received the message loud and clear and acted upon it.

6. Each time another worry begins to aggravate you, follow the same process. Write it down, fold up the paper and pop it into the box.
7. You'll find the worries begin to evaporate and will cease to keep nagging you.
8. At the end of the week, open your box and empty out the pieces of paper. Read through the worries and be pleasantly surprised as you discover that most of them took care of themselves, without requiring any action from you whatsoever.

Remember – most of the things that we worry about never happen!

On a final note, it's important to remember to set aside some time, say thirty minutes each day, to enjoy experiencing some of the relaxation techniques. If you continue to lead a stressful life during the day and simply 'hope' that a quick technique will send you off to sleep at night, you're potentially setting yourself up for failure. Organise yourself properly and get your plan in place. With repetition, your mind will begin to adopt your new relaxed pattern of behaviour and as a consequence it will be much easier to experience those same feelings at night-time.

Case Study: When Love Dies

Betty, seventy-two, came to see me on the recommendation of her son who had come across NLP through a business training course that he'd recently attended.

His father had passed away after a long-term illness almost a year ago and his mother was struggling to come to terms with her life alone, becoming increasingly reclusive as a result. Although she had received bereavement counselling following her husband's death, her son felt she'd benefit from something a bit 'different' to put a spring in her step, a smile on her face and make her feel positive about her future once more.

Betty had been married to Jim for nearly fifty years. They had had a good life together, living in the same village for most of that time, and had two children. Jim had been an active member of the local community, having served as a parish councillor as well as being on the committee of the local golf club – playing golf had been one of his passions. Most of their social life had centred round Jim's interests. Now alone, Betty was struggling to find her feet and felt increasingly lonely and isolated.

It's not uncommon for people who have recently become separated from their partners, for whatever reason, to utter the words, 'I feel as if I'm losing my mind' – for losing a part of their minds is exactly what happens. Not only have they shared a life but also, over time, developed a 'shared mind' or memory bank that stores a record of experiences and anecdotes. Couples who have been together for a long time often finish each other's sentences, fill in missing gaps and correct each other's stories.

When feelings of grief, which could include anger or guilt, get added to this, it can be difficult to pick oneself up and start creating a new life. Understandably, the person is not in the most resourceful state.

Step 1 – Relax: During her first session, I was able to establish that Betty was carrying a huge amount of guilt. During her husband's final months he'd spent a long time in hospital receiving treatment. Betty often asked herself if she could have done more. She replayed in her mind conversations that she'd had with the doctors, panicking that perhaps she'd said the wrong thing at the wrong time and hadn't asked enough questions.

She could not get out of her mind the images of her husband lying in his hospital bed getting weaker each day.

Before I showed Betty how to download any of the NLP apps, we began by working through all the relaxation techniques in Chapter 8. It's very much harder to have a stressed mind if your body is in a relaxed state. I recommended that she spend at least thirty minutes each day going through these.

Step 2 – Banish Bad Pictures: Our next task was to rid her mind of those unpleasant pictures. Betty could still remember sitting at Jim's hospital bed, holding his hand. She was fully 'associated' in this picture – i.e. she felt as if she were sitting on the chair and could see her hands. I asked her to imagine floating up out of her body and moving to the back of the room, by the door. So she became a bystander rather than a participant and could see herself sitting at his bedside, rather than being 'herself'. She noticed the difference in her feelings.

Next, I asked her to take that image and shrink it down. To drain all the colour out of it. And to turn any sounds right down – she could hear the bleeping of the hospital monitor.

Then I asked her to white out that image completely. She had successfully downloaded App 2.

Whilst it's not uncommon to feel that there is just one image in particular that keeps returning to our minds, there are often several. We worked through each one as they came up and not all them came into her mind during the first session. After the first couple of sessions, Betty was able to deal with these pictures herself and during the following week she tackled three or four more images that came to her during the night.

Step 3 – Good Pictures: After she had successfully rid herself of the bad pictures that were haunting her, I helped Betty to download some good pictures – App 1. I asked her to remember a time in the past when Jim was fit and healthy. Could she remember a favourite time of theirs? Betty chose a trip to Paris they had enjoyed: she remembered Jim sitting opposite her at a restaurant on the Champs Elysées – he look tanned, happy and relaxed.

I asked Betty if she was 'in' the picture and so could see all her surroundings, or whether she felt as if she was 'looking' at it. She realised that she wasn't *fully associated* because she could see the outside of the restaurant, the colourful canopy and all the other tables on the pavement – in fact she was looking at herself and her husband.

I asked her to imagine that she was floating into that scene, floating into herself sitting at that table. So now, rather than looking at the two of them sitting at the table, she could actually feel as if she were there. As she did this, she brought herself closer to Jim and could now look down and see her hands holding a knife and fork as they ate lunch.

I asked her to bring that picture closer to her; to make it bigger, brighter, bolder and more colourful, and to increase the volume so that she once again could hear all that she had heard.

As Betty closed her eyes to do this, I asked her to say the word 'Jim' several times, for this would build up a link between the word and the picture. In the future, when she hears his name or thinks it to herself, this happy picture is what will come into her mind.

I told her to consider this to be her special snapshot of Jim. And to notice the good feelings that she feels inside herself as she looks at this picture of him.

Step 4 – An Anchor: Feeling much calmer and more accepting of the situation, Betty wanted to tackle her isolation and lack of confidence. Betty and Jim's social life had revolved around his commitments with the golf club. Just a few years ago when Jim was club secretary, she could remember the fun she had dressing up, attending club functions and feeling she was the centre of attention. She had enjoyed organising fundraising events and social activities for the wives. Now, without Jim at her side, she had lost that social connection and felt she had no place amongst these people. She didn't feel strong enough to start all over again and, indeed, didn't know where to begin.

I showed Betty how to download App 10 – Your Confidence Anchor. She was able to bring to mind several memories of times in the past when she had felt happy and confident:

- A time in the past when she felt good going out with Jim – she remembered wearing a beautiful ballgown at a New Year's Eve dance.
- A time in the past when she went out independently – she had organised a social event for the golf club wives and took them on a shopping trip to London followed by afternoon tea.
- A time in the past when she could not stop laughing – she remembered her grandchildren as they played in the garden.

These memories were 'anchored' to the squeezing of her thumb and middle finger on her dominant hand, giving her a valuable resource to use when she next felt lacking in confidence.

Step 5 – Your Timeline: Because Betty was still struggling to imagine a future without Jim, I suggested we take a walk along her timeline – App 3.

Once we had her timeline established, we talked about the kinds of things she would like to do in the future. She was aware of local groups that she could join in order to meet people, e.g. the local WI, but she didn't feel confident enough to go along to one of these meetings alone.

With Betty standing in the middle of the room, I asked her to imagine her timeline – the past was behind her and her future stretched out in front of her. As she closed her eyes, I asked her to walk forward into next week. And then to stop: keeping her eyes closed, I asked her to take an imaginary look around – what could she see? She told me she could see herself visiting her grandchildren – one of them had a birthday to celebrate and she had been invited to the party.

I asked her to squeeze her thumb and middle finger together to 'fire off her anchor' and allow herself to experience some of those confident feelings inside as she looked forward to this event.

Then, with Betty keeping her eyes closed, I asked her to walk forward one month from now. To take a look around and see what she sees. And again to trigger her confidence anchor.

We repeated this process as she walked two months and then eventually six months down her timeline, each time using the benefit of those boosted confidence feelings inside her.

I then turned Betty around and asked her to walk back to the present day. When she opened her eyes, we discussed what she had seen.

With this new-found confidence inside her, she had 'mentally rehearsed' attending one of the WI events. She had been able to see herself at this event, laughing and chatting to people. It had not looked so scary after all.

One observation had taken her by surprise. She hadn't arrived at this event alone. She had seen herself with a neighbour who lived nearby. They knew each other well enough to stop for a brief chat but had never socialised together before. Betty hadn't thought of her as a potential friend, but seeing her picture there so strongly on that timeline made her realise that she should contact her.

Betty and I continued to work together over a period of three months and gradually she started 'picking up the pieces of her life', as she told me.

I thought it an interesting phrase to use, for as I explained earlier on in this book, as children we learnt how to put jigsaw puzzles together by looking at the picture on the box. The picture was our guide and we gathered up the pieces of the puzzle and made them match the picture.

Our mind works in a similar way – show it a picture and it will work hard to ensure your reality matches that picture as closely as possible. Once Betty had mastered the art of walking along her timeline and creating good pictures, the pieces of her life came together and enabled her to experience many more years of joy.

14

Apps for Your Mind

In this chapter you'll find details of those very special NLP techniques that have been used by highly successful people for many years, plus a couple of my own that I've created. You'll discover, too, that as you begin to familiarise yourself with how your own mind works, you'll also be able to adapt and modify the techniques to suit you better.

I've chunked them down and called them your 'Apps for Your Mind'. So just as you would download an app onto your phone, you can 'download' one of these techniques into your mind, to easily solve whatever problem you may be struggling with.

With each app, I make suggestions as to which problems you can fix, but this is only a suggestion and you can in fact use all the apps to fix your life's problems. Only you will know exactly which or how many apps will be most appropriate for you. You can use as many as you like and, in fact, I would suggest a little experimentation – if what you're doing doesn't seem to be working, try something else.

In NLP there is no failure, only feedback, so downloading your apps with a sense of curiosity is what's going to make them more successful for you.

Give yourself the time and space to work through the techniques, and if some of the visualisation feels like a struggle, go back to Get in the Right State (Chapter 8), and consider doing some of the relaxation exercises first.

Occasionally you may find it easier to go through some of the techniques with a friend or colleague, who'll be able to read out the instructions for you as you relax and work through the stages with your eyes closed.

Remember, this is what I'd be doing with you if you were a client coming to see me.

Congratulations – you are taking that first step towards Fixing Your Life!

APP 1 – Good Pictures, Good Feelings

Uses: **Enhancing good feelings**
Getting rid of bad thoughts and feelings

Note: If you have unhelpful images running through your mind, you might want to download App 2 before you do this one.

As we've already discovered, playing around with the pictures in your mind can rapidly change the feelings you have inside your body. Follow these instructions to start feeling good and notice how your feelings change:

1. Think of a happy time.

2. Become aware of the picture that springs to your mind.

3. Turn the colour up, making it stronger, brighter and bolder.

4. Bring it closer to you now, so it's right up there in front of you.

5. If there are any sounds in this image of yours, turn the volume up.

6. Turn it into a movie now, have the image moving.

7. Make the colours and sounds stronger again.

8. Notice how this changes your feelings.

9. Become aware of where exactly you're seeing that picture –

    to the left, to the right, high up, low down, etc.

Whenever you feel in need of a pick-me-up, insert good pictures into your mind. Once you are aware of the position of your picture, you'll be able to glance at it from time to time throughout your day, making you feel better.

APP 2 – Banish Bad Pictures

**Uses: Getting rid of bad thoughts to change your feelings
Putting a halt to replaying bad episodes over and
over**

If this is your first attempt at ridding yourself of bad images, pick an example that is not too traumatic. Once you have an understanding of this process, you'll be able to deal with other, more unpleasant situations. For rather more serious and traumatic events seek the help of a qualified NLP practitioner.

Can you think of a minor disagreement that you had recently? Are you playing it over and over in your mind? If so:

1. Take yourself back to that irritating moment.

2. Notice where the picture is positioned.

3. Is it in colour or black and white?

4. Are there any sounds?

5. And what about the size?

6. Does it have a border around it?

Now let's change pictures:

1. Shrink that picture down.

2. Turn it into black and white.

3. Turn the volume down so you can no longer hear those voices.

4. Move that picture further and further away.

5. Shrink it right down into a dot.

6. And now imagine taking a paintbrush and painting it white.

7. White it out.

8. And notice how this changes your feelings.

Always remember that good pictures in our minds create good feelings and bad pictures create bad feelings.

Follow this up with App 1 and you'll begin to feel very much better.

APP 3 – Discovering Your Timeline

Uses: Will enable you to think about your past, present and future more easily

Most of us spend our time thinking about our pasts (even if it is about things that happened five minutes ago), or about our futures (things that are going to happen).

Our minds code time in the context of the past, present and future and we spend our time directing our thoughts in one direction or another. We don't all do this in the same way, so learning how you personally code time will enable you to travel along your timeline to your advantage.

Travelling along your timeline enables you to:

- Test out new ideas to check that they are sound.

- Predict potential problems and pitfalls.

- Mentally rehearse a situation or a particular skill

- Overcome fears

- Move forward if you feel stuck in the past

Allow yourself plenty of time to relax and think about these events. There's no need to rush this activity.

1. Think back to a birthday you had ten years ago. Take a few moments to decide which birthday you're going to remember.

2. Notice the picture that springs to your mind as you think about this birthday.

3. As those memories start flooding back, could you become aware enough of that picture to be able to point to it?

4. Now think back to your last birthday – again notice where you feel you are seeing that picture and point to it once more.

5. Now think about your next birthday – how old you will be and what you might be doing. Notice where that picture seems to appear.

6. Now think about your birthday in five years' time. Again, how old will you be then, where might you be and who with? Are you getting an imaginary picture? Point to it.

7. And how about your birthday in ten years' time?

8. Imagine drawing a line from the first birthday you thought of, through the second and the third, all the way to the one you'll be having in ten years' time.

9. This is your timeline. Now extend it further back into the past and further forward into the future.

Some people have timelines with their pasts behind them and their futures in front of them. In these instances their timelines may feel as if they are running through them, as if they are standing on the line itself.

For others, the line could feel as if it comes over their shoulder and runs at a slight angle.

Others may have a V-shaped line with their past coming up the left-hand line up to the present (which is where the two lines meet) and then their future shoots off along the right-hand side.

It's also possible to have a slightly more unusual configuration, such as a future that heads up towards the sky or a past that seems to go down into the ground. There is no wrong or right timeline – it's just the way you code your memories and the concept of your future. It's possible for your timeline to change – if you do this exercise today and repeat it in six months' time, it could be different.

Take a few moments to gather some more information about your timeline:

- Is it short or long?

- Does it feel heavy or light?

- Is the future higher or lower than the past?

- Are there any sounds on your timeline, or is it quiet?

- Is it large or small – could you feel it envelop you or is it a thin line?

- Is yours in colour or black and white?

Time Travel:

1. Take a piece of string or ribbon and lay it on the floor in the same direction that you saw your timeline.

2. Place yourself on the line, in the place where you feel the present is.

3. Notice how much of the line is now behind you and how much is in front of you.

4. Do you have more of a past than a future? Or the other way around?

Remember – there is no wrong or right answer to this but it's an interesting observation.

Some people get bogged down in the past and find it difficult to visualise their future. Physically walking along their timeline to travel into the future can really help here.

And others get so future-oriented, always dreaming up new ideas, that they can fail to see potential pitfalls along the way. Travelling back along their timeline can help them to remember why certain schemes failed in the past and also help them to avoid repeating mistakes.

APP 4 – Hindsight in Your Foresight

Uses: Will give you the ability to test out your ideas and anticipate potential problems

Note: Before you download this app, you will first need to have downloaded App 3 – Discovering Your Timeline.

1. As you stand on your timeline in the present moment, think of an appointment, meeting or social engagement that you have coming up in the future that has given you a few feelings of anxiety.

2. Close your eyes and begin to take some steps forward along your timeline. Keep walking into the future, until you reach the point where this meeting takes place.

3. Have a good look around (in your imagination) – see what you see, hear what you hear and feel what you might feel. As you keep your eyes closed, notice everything about this meeting that you need to notice.

4. And when you feel you have seen enough, open your eyes and come back down your timeline to the present moment once more.

Now reflect on your experience. What was the outcome of that situation? Did everything go just as you would have liked it to?

If not, what could you do with more of – more confidence, calmness, optimism, concentration? If you could have had the scenario go just the way you wanted it to, what would you have changed? What would you have done differently?

Now, with the benefit of hindsight in your foresight, think about which of the other apps you should download before that meeting of yours happens for real. What other resources should you acquire in time for this event – a new outfit, perhaps? Could you 'consult an expert': is there anyone you could talk to who has successfully come through what you're about to go through?

APP 5 – Decision-maker

Uses: **Torn between two decisions? Test out each scenario on your timeline and then make the decision**

Note: Before downloading this Decision-maker, you'll need to first download App 3 – Discovering Your Timeline.

1. Get a feel for your timeline, laying your string or ribbon down on the floor.

2. Step into the present moment.

3. Think about Option Number One – getting a good picture in your mind.

4. Close your eyes and walk down your timeline to experience your future if you decide to go with this option.

5. Take yourself forward as far as you feel you need to – next week, next month, next year.

6. As you arrive in your future, notice everything around you – see what you see, hear what you hear and feel what you would feel.

7. When you have finished taking in all this information, turn around and travel back down your timeline to the present once more, opening your eyes.

8. At this point, hop off your line and make some handwritten notes about what you experienced.

9. Hop back on your timeline, making sure you're standing in the present.

10. Think about Option Number Two – getting a good picture in your mind.

11. Walk down your timeline, closing your eyes once more, to experience the future if you decide to go with Option Two.

12. Again, notice everything around you – see what you see, hear what you hear and feel what you would feel.

13. When you have finished taking in all this information, turn around and travel down your timeline once more to the present moment, opening your eyes.

14. Again, hop off your timeline and make a few notes about what you experienced.

15. Compare the outcome of Option One to Option Two. Decision-making should be much easier now.

APP 6 – A Dose of Reality

Uses: Testing out your big ideas

Note: Before downloading this app, you'll need to have first downloaded App 3 – Discovering Your Timeline.

Some of us can be so 'future-oriented', with heads filled with dreams and big ideas, that we can fail to notice the present and easily forget the past. Whilst there's nothing wrong in being focused on the future, this one-dimensional view of the world can result in us failing to see the long-term implications of our actions.

Test out your big idea:

1. Arrange your timeline ribbon or tape on the floor. Establish where you feel the present moment is and stand on it.

2. Look off into the future and see your 'big idea' taking shape. Allow a picture to form in the distance of your new reality, should this big idea come to fruition.

3. Move closer to it. And keep noticing what you notice.

4. As you continue to look at your new future from this slight distance, become aware of something growing behind it.

5. It may help to visualise this as smoke or clouds initially, becoming more solid just behind your new future.

6. As you see that hazy image take shape and grow in size till it begins to dwarf your original picture, walk closer to it.

7. Walk towards your 'big idea' and keep walking through it.

8. The hazy image behind your 'big idea' is the future of your future. The result or consequence of your big idea becoming a reality.

9. Step into this 'future future' and close your eyes. With your eyes closed, you'll be able to have a good 'look' around you. See what you see, hear what you hear and feel what you would feel.

10. Gain as much information and knowledge as you feel you need.

11. Turn around, travel back down your timeline to the present moment once more and open your eyes.

12. Step off the timeline and reflect on what you experienced.

APP 7 – Leaving the Past Behind

Uses: Ideal for creating a shift if you feel stuck in the past

Note: Before downloading this app, you'll need to have first downloaded App 3 – Discovering Your Timeline.

Just as some people can find themselves only able to focus on a future (see App 6 – A Dose of Reality), others can find themselves only able to access their pasts. This is fine if the past is filled with memories of success, achievement and happiness, but sometimes traumatic events can leave us feeling overwhelmed and lacking in energy to move forwards.

Some timelines have the past spread out in front of the person – either from side to side or straight out ahead – this makes it much harder to see a future.

Experiment by changing your timeline around. It's important to view this as an experiment to see how comfortable you feel with it. You can always put it back the way it was before you started if you prefer.

1. Standing still, allow yourself to be comfortable with the present moment – think about getting up this morning, brushing your teeth, eating breakfast and all the other things you did between then and now.

2. Now think about yesterday – what you did – and as you do, take a step backwards. Pause here.

3. Now think about last week – and take a step back.

4. And last month – take a step back. Pause.

5. And six months ago. Take a step back and pause.

6. Now we're going to start moving forward in time.

7. Step forward from six months to one month ago. See what you saw a moment ago.

8. And again step forward from one month to one week ago and again experience here what you did as you travelled back in time.

9. And again step forward from one week ago to the present moment.

10. And step forward again – this time into tomorrow. Think about what you'll be doing tomorrow.

11. And step forward again – into next week. Think only about the mundane activities you'll be doing – brushing your teeth, supermarket shopping, etc.

12. And again step forward – this time into next month. Which month will it be? What will the weather be like?

13. If the future has a habit of seeming a little daunting and difficult to visualise, just give your image a rosy glow. There's no need to fill in the details at this point. All you need to do is to give yourself a good feeling about it at this stage. Enjoy experiencing this future moment of yours.

14. And then you can turn around and step back down your line to the present moment. And stop.

You'll be able to repeat this activity, but next time, begin at the present and allow yourself to move into the future only.

Practising this each day or even several times a day will enable you to order your timeline in a way that is more helpful to you (e.g. past behind and future in front). Each time you do it, you'll be able to lengthen it a little more – move from next month to three months down the line and then six months. You can move as quickly or as slowly as you want to down your line.

Remember, if the future looks a little worrying, you can always download some of the other apps to help you to move forward into it. What resources do you think you'll need to acquire to be successful?

APP 8 – Instant Gratification

Uses: Increasing staying power for long-term goals

Note: Before downloading this app, you'll need to have first downloaded App 3 – Discovering Your Timeline.

It's not uncommon for our long-term goals to sometimes feel as if they are becoming a more distant reality as we struggle to keep on track and motivated to continue the pursuit of them. A significant weight-loss goal, for example, is going to require a good deal of determination over a long period of time. As does saving up for an expensive item such as a holiday or a home. But if you could begin to experience all the benefits of achieving that goal a little in advance, wouldn't it make it easier for you?

The more compelling and desirable you can crank up your future to be, the more likely you are to resist that extra piece of chocolate cake or another trip to the shops or pub.

1. Arrange your timeline ribbon or tape on the floor. Establish where you feel the present moment is and stand on it.

2. Look off into the future and see your 'goal' out there. Allow an image to begin forming in your mind and notice all that you can about it.

3. Is it in colour? Are there any sounds? Can you feel warmth or a breeze?

4. Allow that image of your bright, new, shiny future when you have reached your goal to become bigger.

5. Step along your timeline and reach that wonderful moment. Your wonderful future when everything that you've been working and striving for is finally yours.

6. Close your eyes and literally allow this atmosphere to envelop you as you begin to enjoy being who you are going to become.

7. Notice everything you can about this feeling – this feeling of stepping into your future. See what you see, hear what you hear and feel how good this future of yours feels.

8. Take a look around – what do you see? What colours, sounds, smells? Who do you see – people that you know or new people that you've yet to meet?

9. Enjoy this moment.

10. When you are ready, you may open your eyes and travel back down your timeline, to the present moment.

11. Standing in the present moment now, reflect on how your determination and motivation have changed. Will this new energy help you to stay on track?

APP 9 – Creating a 'New You'

Uses: Starting over again (broken relationships, job losses)
Restoring your self-image

1. Take a few moments to relax, close your eyes and just allow your imagination to take over.

2. Think about how you would look if you were as confident and outgoing as you'd like to be.

3. Make that image of yourself a little larger and notice everything about the 'new you'. How do you walk? How do you talk? What sort of places do you go to? What about your clothes? And what about the expression on your face?

4. Once you've got a nice, clear picture of how you'd like to be, make a little movie of yourself doing all the kinds of things you'd like to be doing. Make that image larger and make the colours brighter and bolder. Make the sounds louder and the feelings stronger.

5. Now, imagine floating up out of your body and floating down into the 'you' inside that movie clip. It feels a little like slipping into a new set of clothes.

6. Enjoy this moment of being the 'new you'.

7. Now open your eyes once more and imagine how it would be if you woke up tomorrow with your life beginning to go exactly as in that clip.

8. What did you notice? Is there anything you can do to help yourself along to becoming that new you?

Repeat this exercise several times over a period of a week. Notice how the 'new you' changes and develops during that time.

APP 10 – Your Confidence Anchor

Uses: **Extra-confident feelings for interviews, public speaking, presentations, performing on stage, social situations and meeting new people**

Note: Chapter 5 gives you further details about how anchoring works. As this exercise requires you to close your eyes you can either read through all the instructions before you begin, ensuring you'll understand all the steps, or you can invite a friend or colleague to read through the exercise for you. You'll be asked to squeeze your thumb and middle finger together – for this exercise you'll need to use those on your dominant hand, i.e. the one that you write with.

1. Take a few moments to find somewhere comfortable to sit and make yourself relaxed.

2. Remind yourself of a time in the past when you felt really confident. Perhaps this was a time at work when you were praised for doing something well, a time in the past when you exuded so much confidence that you actually surprised yourself.

3. Close your eyes and take yourself back to that time. See all that you saw, hear all that you heard and feel the feelings that you felt back then.

4. Become aware of what you're seeing in that picture, and make it a bit bigger. Turn the colours up brighter, bolder and stronger, and if there are any sounds in this memory of yours, turn the volume up louder.

5. Make that picture bigger and bring it closer to you.

6. If you can see yourself in that picture (i.e. you're disso-ciated), imagine floating up from your chair and sliding down into the 'you' in that picture.

7. Become the *you* and really enjoy this moment once more.

8. Enjoy this time in the past when you truly felt confident, positive and in control about something.

9. As you continue to enjoy looking at this picture, become aware of where exactly in your body you're experiencing those feelings of confidence. Are they in your big toe, for example? Or at the end of your nose? Most probably not – where are they exactly?

10. Locate those feelings and make them spin around even faster, allowing them to spread right through your body from the top of your head to the tips of your toes.

11. Keep running through these steps until you feel that wonderful feeling begin to peak.

12. As it becomes stronger and stronger, just squeeze together the thumb and middle finger on your dominant hand. Squeeze them together tightly, capturing all of those good, good feelings.

13. And release. Relax and open your eyes as you come back into the room.

14. Whenever you want to feel this confident feeling again, all you're going to have to do is squeeze that thumb and middle finger together once more.

Running through this exercise several times a day will ensure that your 'confident anchor' becomes more powerful. Repetition is the key to getting this anchor really powerful.

You can intensify the feelings attached to this anchor by remembering to squeeze that same thumb and middle finger together whenever you find yourself experiencing other confident moments. Do it as it happens.

Once you have established this anchor, you'll be able to summon up those same good feelings automatically, simply by squeezing that thumb and middle finger once more – whenever you need it.

The NLP Anchoring Techniques are featured here with the kind permission of Richard Bandler

APP 11 – Supersize Your Confidence

Uses: Looking and sounding confident.

Your Confident Voice: We all have many voices inside our heads – there are our happy, relaxed voices and our grumpy, cross voices. We use a different voice at home when speaking to loved ones from the one we might use at work with our colleagues and boss. We switch and change our voices to suit the situations we find ourselves in, to make them sound more appropriate.

Altering the sound of our voice is something that we naturally do throughout the day. And if we can do this spontaneously and naturally, there's no reason why we can't learn how to do this deliberately.

1. Can you think of someone whose voice you admire? What is it about their voice – the intonation, depth, pitch, their accent or the speed with which they talk? This could be a friend of yours or someone from TV or the movies.

2. Start running that person's voice through your mind. Remember when you last heard it. Did you have a conversation with that person or did you hear them on the radio? Keep listening and running that voice over and over till you've got a good sense of what makes it special.

3. Get a newspaper or magazine and starting reading an article in your mind, using that voice. Imagine that voice

running through your mind as your eyes follow those words on the page.

4. Start with just a couple of sentences to begin with and then keep repeating them till you feel you've perfected it. The voice inside your head, reading those words, sounds just like the person you originally thought of.

5. Now start to read those same sentences out loud, matching your voice with theirs. Keep running that voice through your mind as you speak out loud. Repeat this several times.

6. Notice what you notice as your own voice begins to match that voice on the inside. What did you change? What makes it better? What works? What doesn't work?

Practise doing this a few times and you'll learn what it is you need to do to make your voice sound more confident and appealing than perhaps it ever has before.

Your Confident Body: We've all come across people who simply seem to exude an air of confidence, whatever the circumstances. Something about the way that they move or stride across a room perhaps? Or their posture and the way they move their hands? That flick of the hair or the sparkle in the eyes. What is it about them that makes them come across as confident to you? What makes them stand out from the crowd?

1. Think of someone who has that effect on you. Someone who when you look at them, you just know that they're feeling confident on the inside. It can be someone you know personally – a friend or colleague – or someone you've seen on TV or in a movie.

2. Now stand up and imagine that person standing in front of you right now. There they are, right up close. Have a good look them – how they move, their body language, their posture. Make that image in front of you really life-like. Turn the colours up brighter, bolder and stronger – really noticing every detail of this person.

3. Now imagine turning that person around, so they are no longer looking at you, but are facing the other way as you stand behind them.

4. Step forward and, as you do, feel yourself stepping inside their body – it's a bit like slipping into a new suit of clothes. Become that person as you climb into them.

5. Shuffle around and make yourself comfortable inside this new body. Feel what you feel and notice what you notice.

6. How do you hold your arms and move your hands, for example? How are you standing? Notice if you're taller now.

7. Take a few steps forward inside this body and become comfortable with moving around like a confident person.

You'll now know what changes you need to make to appear as confident as them.

Anchor Your Confidence: As you enjoy using this body and testing out that new voice of yours, remember to anchor these good feelings – App 10 – by squeezing together the thumb and middle finger of your dominant hand. Supersize your 'Confidence Anchor'.

APP 12 – Circle of Excellence

Uses: Teaches you how to 'mentally rehearse' a future situation, such as an interview, audition or presentation, without the usual accompanying feelings of nervousness

To help you get through personal situations such as visiting in-laws or returning goods to a store

1. Create a circle on the floor. You can use a piece of string, draw a chalk circle or use a hoop, whatever's easiest for you.

2. Think of the situation that's coming up in the future and take a few moments to consider its aspects – who will be there, where it will be, how much time there will be, what your desired outcome is.

3. Decide what resources or skills you'll need. For example, an interview will require you to be confident and able to think freely; a meeting with in-laws may require you to be calm; registering a complaint may require you to be assertive, knowledgeable and quick-thinking.

4. Think about your breathing and posture. Have a good picture in your mind of how you'd like to handle the situation.

5. Now, recall a time in the past when you handled a situation in just the way you'd like this one to go, when you had all the resources that you'll be needing this time.

6. Step into your magic circle, close your eyes and relive that time again. See what you saw, hear what you heard, feel what you felt and make that image in your mind grow and grow. As the picture grows, so too will your feelings.

7. Squeeze together the thumb and middle finger on your dominant hand, capturing all of those good feelings there.

8. Relax your hand and step out of your circle.

9. Think of another feeling or resource you'll be needing to handle this future situation well. Search back through your memories once more to remember a time in the past when you had exactly that resource.

10. Step back into your circle again and run through Step 6 once more, with this new memory.

11. Step back out of your circle.

12. Relax and think of all the other resources and feelings you'll be needing to get that future event running just the way you'd like it to go.

13. Hop back into your circle and run through Step 6 once more.

14. Come back out of the circle.

15. Once you have gathered together and anchored all the resources and feelings you want to be with you at this event, jump back into your circle once.

16. Close your eyes and visualise that event going just the way you'd like it to. As you squeeze your thumb and middle finger together once more, you'll be able to experience these feelings of excellence as you mentally rehearse your situation. See what you'll be wearing; see all the other people there; notice your posture, your composure, the tone of your voice, your feelings of inner strength.

17. Imagine your circle has a colour – a good strong colour – one that represents confidence and success to you.

18. Imagine this colour rising up in a mist all around you – as it travels up, enveloping you, imagine it swirling around all the way to the top of your head and beyond.

19. Add a bit of stardust to it.

When you experience the situation you were thinking about for real, just squeeze that thumb and middle finger together again, and all these resourceful feelings will flood your body once more. This will enable you to handle the situation in just the way you wanted to.

APP 13 – Your Portable Mirror

Uses: **Presentations**
Public speaking
Speeches
Interviews
Performances

I've long been fascinated by the fact that, in the privacy of our own homes, we can behave like different people.

For example, most of us sing better – just compare the voice you sing with in the shower to the one you'd come out with if you had to sing in public. How many of us are blessed with two left feet on the dance floor but can easily pirouette and perform graceful movements around our sitting rooms? And think of the quality of conversations you've had with yourself in the mirror!

When no one's looking, we can move more confidently, speak more confidently and express ideas and opinions that perhaps we'd usually keep to ourselves.

There are various techniques that can be used to help get over the fear of standing up in front of an audience – focusing on just one member of the audience perhaps, looking up into the space above the audience, or imagining that there are just five people there.

But how good would it be if you couldn't see any of them? How good would it be if you could be back in the privacy of your home – just you and a mirror? How wonderful would it be to have your own personal, portable mirror that you could put between yourself and your audience? Your personal protection, a safety barrier almost, blocking them out.

1. Stand in front of a mirror and bring with you all the resources you acquired in Apps 10 and 11.

2. Adopt your posture of confidence, use that voice of confidence and bring on a liberal sprinkling of your star quality.

3. Now is your opportunity to rehearse the performance or talk that you'll be giving, with no one watching.

4. Run through your speech or your lines and watch yourself in the mirror.

5. Are you happy with your performance? Would you like to adjust it? Notice what you notice. What works well? What would you like more of? What would you like less of?

6. Turn the volume up on your voice – that voice of confidence. Really enjoy using this voice.

7. Accentuate your movements or posture. Remember that in some instances keeping still will be better, so give off that confident air even through your stillness.

8. As you look at yourself in the mirror, remind yourself that no one's watching. This is your opportunity to be the 'you'

that you've always wanted to be and give the performance of your life.

9. Enjoy this moment and as you do – squeeze together that thumb and middle finger on your dominant hand. You'll be capturing the 'essence' of your performance into that anchor of yours, ready to use when you need it.

10. Run through your performance at least three times and as many as you feel you need to completely and utterly perfect it.

11. As you see your image in that mirror, allow yourself to see a gentle haze of people sitting behind your reflection. In your foreground, you'll see yourself and in the background, you'll see that haze. Relax and enjoy.

12. Do this at least once a day for a week before your performance.

On the day:
1. As you step on the stage or in front of your audience or stand up to give your presentation to that group of people, fire off your anchor – squeeze that thumb and middle finger together once more and notice what happens.

2. Your magic mirror will pop up in front of you – blocking out the audience, allowing you to only see yourself.

3. Looking at yourself in that mirror once more, you'll be able to give that performance of a lifetime – the performance you'd be giving in the privacy of your own home.

4. In the background, you may see that gentle haze of people, but your image in the foreground is what will drive you on to being the 'you' you'd wanted to be.

APP 14 – Stop Blushing Now

Uses: **Presentations**
Public speaking
Confrontational situations

Blushing and embarrassment go hand in hand. We've all experienced those moments of self-consciousness that can trigger a reddening of the skin, most usually on the face.

Blushing from embarrassment is connected to your 'fight-or-flight' response. As you find yourself in an awkward situation, your body automatically releases a rush of adrenaline that then causes your breathing and heart rate to speed up, enabling you to run away from this perceived danger, if you need to.

Adrenaline also causes your blood vessels to dilate in order to improve blood flow and oxygen delivery and this is the case with blushing. The veins in your face dilate and as more blood flows through them, your face becomes red.

If you regularly blush, or have an event coming up, such as public speaking, you'll be able to plan in advance. Reducing your overall anxiety levels will help you to keep control over your adrenaline.

Your Success Plan:
1. Check out Chapter 8, 'Get in the Right State', and follow the relaxation techniques.

2. Supersize your confidence and create an anchor – Apps 10 and 11 – ready to activate during the upcoming situation.

These strategies are going to be really useful if you are able to plan in advance. However, most of us fall into blushing episodes accidentally – and what are you going to do if it starts to happen spontaneously and you need to get a grip on it?

Your Emergency Plan: As we've already discovered, our internal dialogue (the little voice inside your head that rarely keeps quiet – yes, that one!) can have an enormous effect on our well-being and actions.

Think back to the last time you blushed. Can you remember what you were saying to yourself? Usually people's internal dialogue goes something along the lines of, 'Oh no, I think I'm going to go red. Yes, I am, I just know it – I'm turning red. I hope they don't notice my face going red. I can feel it – it's starting to turn red. Great, last thing I wanted – my face going red!'

I'm sure you can see now exactly why your face did turn red. Your internal dialogue issued a 'command', your mind created a picture for you and your body followed – doing exactly as you told it to.

Step 1 – Change Your Words: Next time you feel yourself starting to get that rush of adrenaline that signals to you that your face might start turning red, issue a command of a different sort.

'I think I'm turning BLUE – yes, I am – I'm turning BLUE. I can feel that BLUENESS start to spread now across my face, my chest and down my arms even – I'm turning BLUE!'

As it's usual to feel heat rising up our faces, instruct this feeling to travel in a downwards direction:

> *'I can feel the BLUE start to drain down from the top of my head, down through my face, my eyes, my cheeks . . . down my neck, my shoulders, my chest. Yes, I'm definitely turning BLUE.'*

Test this out – it works!

Step 2 – Change Your Pictures: As well as our words, we know that the pictures created by our minds have a very powerful effect on our bodies. So, if you need more help – use your visualisation skills.

Most people caught in an embarrassing flush will automatically begin to create pictures and start imagining how red they must be looking. So, even if they aren't red in the cheeks, they soon will be. Start creating pictures of a different kind:

1.   Imagine a giant ice-cube sitting on the top of your head.

2.   Slowly it begins to cool you right down.

3.   Notice how the ice starts to melt.

4.   Ice-cold water dripping down your head, your face, your cheeks.

Test this out and notice what happens.

You can now quickly and easily get yourself out of any difficult situations just by combining these two techniques. The good thing is no one else can see what you're thinking, so put your imagination to good use.

As you increasingly begin to gain control in the kind of situations that would previously have caused you problems, you'll find yourself becoming more and more relaxed. And as you relax more and more, you'll quickly discover that blushing is a thing of the past.

APP 15 – Your Motivation Anchor

Uses: **Getting new projects off the ground**
Getting on with unpleasant tasks (tax return, weeding the garden)
Keeping enthusiasm up if you hit a plateau (weight loss)

Note: Chapter 5 discusses anchoring in more detail.

Although your mind may have clear, concrete evidence that things just have to change – such as needing to lose weight, quit smoking or take up an exercise programme – it can sometimes still feel like making any kind of change is going to be an uphill struggle.

It can be all too easy to convince yourself that you're just not the kind of person who has the energy and strength required to make those changes . . . but somewhere in your life you do in fact have the motivation it's going to take – it can just get a little hidden sometimes.

So let's take a few moments to gather up all your motivational energy from those area of your life where you already have it and use it here to propel you forward.

As with all the techniques, read through the instructions carefully before trying them out on yourself. Find somewhere relaxing and quiet to spend these valuable ten minutes.

1. Think of something that you are already motivated to do, even if it's just watching your favourite soap on TV. How motivated are you to ensure that you don't miss the next episode? And how about that buzz of excitement when there's a cliffhanger of an episode? How motivated are you to meet up with friends at the weekend or to rush home from work to relax in the bath? There are things in your life right now that you need no extra persuasion to do. Think about those areas now. And it's OK to simply imagine something fantastic happening – how motivated would you be to collect your winnings if you won the lottery, for example? How motivated would you be if your favourite movie star called you up and invited you out for dinner?

2. Imagine that happening right here and now – seeing it through your own eyes. See what you would see, hear what you would hear and feel exactly how being motivated feels. As you run that scene through in your mind, make all the colours stronger, bolder and brighter. Turn the sounds up even louder. And really enjoy this moment – enjoy feeling really motivated. The more you run this image through in your mind, the stronger the feelings will become – do it at least three times. Become aware of where inside your body you begin to feel that buzz of excitement and make it spin faster. And when you get a good sense of the feelings building in intensity, just *squeeze together your thumb and middle finger* on your dominant hand, capturing all of those good feelings there. After a few moments

of squeezing, you can relax your hand, open your eyes, stand up and shake your body out.

3. Now it's time to attach all of these good, strong, motivated feelings to that new way of behaving – to that new habit, to whatever it is you'd like to be doing. Close your eyes, relax and take yourself on a little journey into the future – a future that involves you being fitter, healthier, happier whatever it is that you'd like to be. See yourself doing exactly what you've been struggling to do, but this time, as you do, squeeze that thumb and middle finger together once more. As those feelings of motivation begin to flood your body, you'll see yourself doing that activity but this time with enjoyment. Notice the expression on your face – see the smile that tells you all is well – and the spring in your step as you move around with more energy than you've felt for a very long time. See what you'll see, hear what you'll hear and feel how good it feels.

4. Keep running this image through your mind, over and over, and as you do, squeeze those fingers tightly once more, attaching all those good feelings you felt earlier to this new activity. Really enjoy this experience.

The more you run this exercise through in your mind, the more motivated you'll become. Again, remember your body produces the kind of sensations it feels are appropriate to the images in your mind. Fantastic pictures mean fantastic feelings.

Watching a sad movie can make your eyes tear up even though you know the events are not happening for real. In the same way, your body will respond to the positive images you put in your mind, leaving you feeling ten times more motivated!

APP 16 – Swish Those Bad Habits Away

Uses: **Controlling impulsive behaviour**
Changing bad habits

Swish is a technique developed by Richard Bandler that
works well to stamp out bad habits or behaviours that we find
ourselves engaging in compulsively. Too many times we find
ourselves automatically doing something, and then regretting
that it happened so quickly that we didn't have time to make
the choice to do something different. Our actions are a result
of our internal pictures – change the pictures and you can
change your actions.

Each piece of compulsive behaviour is accompanied by
several steps – first of all, you get a thought in your mind
that produces a picture. Let's say you get a desire to eat
something and up pops a picture of a chocolate biscuit. This
is quickly followed by a picture of you eating it – perhaps
you'll get a sense of its taste and smell. With this in your
mind, you act compulsively and reach into the cupboard to
help yourself. This process happens so quickly that there
isn't really time for you to think about making a better
decision. We are magnetically drawn to the pictures in our
minds.

With this technique, we'll be attaching a different picture to
the thought, which will then act as your 'decision'.

Make a nice big picture in your mind of how you'd like to
be behaving.

- If it's avoiding chocolate biscuits, perhaps you'll see your-self drinking a glass of water instead.

- If it's saying no to cigarettes, perhaps you'll see yourself walking past your usual tobacconist's, rather than nipping in to buy some.

- If you want to stop biting your nails, perhaps your new picture will be one of you painting your lovely, long nails in a coloured varnish.

We'll be using the good picture to override the faulty program-ming of your bad decision, which is currently driven by a bad picture. In the future, you'll find your desire for the unwanted habit or behaviour will have diminished because the 'new behaviour' picture will automatically accompany your 'crav-ing' picture and will make your decision.

This will help you to choose more wisely – you'll feel as if you are operating on autopilot.

1. Think about the very last thing you are aware of before acting compulsively. If it's eating that biscuit, it might be the sight of the tin, the packet or even your fingers coming up to your mouth as you hold the biscuit between your fingers.

2. Make sure you are fully associated with this picture (i.e. you are seeing your hands and seeing through your eyes, rather than looking at yourself).

3. Make sure your picture is an accurate representation of exactly what happens just before you commit this sin. Notice everything you need to notice about it.

4. Now let's temporarily get that picture out of your mind. Shake your body out to erase it.

5. Call back into your mind that picture of success – of you behaving the way you'd like to. Look at it carefully, take a few moments to fill in all the details. Be precise – what exactly do you want to be doing instead?

6. Now imagine this 'success picture' of yours sliding out of view to your left. And leave it here.

7. Once again call back that image of your bad habit – the one where you carry out that unwanted behaviour.

8. Look at it closely.

9. Then say the word 'swish' out loud and, as you do, have your 'success picture' quickly slide across the bad picture, pushing it out of the way completely, so you can no longer see it. All you see is success.

10. Now repeat this process.

11. Slide your good picture off to the left. Bring your 'bad habit picture' back into view and again, saying 'swish'

out loud, have your success picture bash it out of the way. Send that bad picture way off somewhere where you'll no longer be able to see it. Enjoy looking at success.

12. Repeat this again.

13. Do this five times.

14. Finish up by taking a moment to enjoy looking at your success picture and your newly installed habit.

I would recommend you repeat this technique a couple of times a day for the next few days. Be creative with your images – some people find it effective to imagine their pictures painted onto pieces of glass, so that when the good picture pushes the bad picture away, the glass can shatter into smithereens.

You can also change the position of your pictures – I've suggested the good picture is on the left and moves to the right, but if it feels better for you the other way round then change it. Some people place their good pictures behind their bad pictures, so the good image zooms towards them. You can experiment a little to see what works best for you.

If for some reason you find yourself struggling to achieve change, question your beliefs. How strongly do you really believe that you will be able to quit those cigarettes or get slim enough to fit into those jeans? Go back to 'The Power of Belief' (Chapter 6).

This NLP Swish Pattern is featured here with the kind permission of Richard Bandler

APP 17 – In Two Minds

Uses: **Procrastination**
Decision-making

It's common to feel 'in two minds' about certain things because two minds is exactly what we have – our conscious mind and our subconscious mind.

Sometimes we feel as if we know exactly what we want to achieve on the outside, but that our inside is almost 'sabotaging' our attempts.

How many of us want, on the one hand, to lose weight but, on the other, also really fancy that extra piece of chocolate cake?

Have you ever wanted to travel and explore far-flung countries, but on the other hand felt safer and more comfortable staying at home?

Have you ever wanted to join the local gym, but on the other hand would rather avoid the embarrassment of the changing rooms?

Success becomes much harder to achieve when there's a little bit of an internal struggle going on. It feels as though you are being pulled in two directions and even though both sides want the best for you these feelings can have a sabotaging effect and hold you back. Always keep in mind your ultimate goal – what would you really like to happen? What is your dream?

1. Take a few moments to identify any conflicting thoughts that you may have been experiencing about changing a

particular habit. You may want to take a few moments and write them down on a piece of paper.

2. Once you have done this, place your hands out in front of you. Keep your elbows tucked in to the sides of your body and have your palms facing up to the ceiling.

3. Imagine the part that wants to change this habit for you in one hand (use your dominant hand) and the other part, the bit that sometimes holds you back, in your other (non-dominant) hand.

4. Look at the first hand and imagine you are seeing a shrunken-down movie of you taking the positive action that will lead you towards your goal.

5. Ask this 'part' of you what its positive intention is. Why does it wants you to achieve this goal? Spend a few moments doing this.

6. Then look across to the other hand – the hand with the part of you that holds you back from achieving this goal. This is the part that wants you to do something else instead.

7. Again, see a shrunken-down movie of you taking the negative action that will hold you back from achieving your goal.

8. And ask this part what its positive intention is for you. Why is it that it doesn't want you to take the positive action? What is it trying to achieve for you?

9. Keep running through this process, even if it feels a little strange to begin with. Continue to have this conversation in your mind with both of those parts until it is clear that they both want very similar things for you – they both want you to be happy and secure, even if they have different ideas about how to achieve it.

10. Imagine a new 'super-part' emerging in the space in between your hands. A 'super-part' that has the resources to keep both of those other parts happy and still create success for you. How has this 'super-part' managed to do that? What did it say to achieve that balance? What compromise did it strike?

11. Perhaps it recognised that your habit either gave you pleasure or ensured you avoided potentially stressful situations. What did your 'super-part' suggest to you that would keep your 'bad habit' part and your 'good habit' part equally happy?

12. As you look down into this space in between your hands where your 'super-part' is, perhaps you could give it a colour – a special colour – one that feels right for you. A colour that represents success.

13. Now, moving quickly, bring your hands together and allow those two separate parts to merge with the super-part and become one.

14. Raise your clasped hands to your chest and bring them in to you, allowing this new 'super-part' to become fully absorbed and integrated as a new part of you.

15. Close your eyes and enjoy this feeling of having every bit of your body in agreement about the kind of future you'll have.

As you repeat this technique, you'll discover that all those feelings of internal conflict begin to simply disappear as your mind creatively begins to provide you with solutions that will fit the bill and satisfy all parts of you.

If you find yourself struggling to keep that part of you that wants to hold you back satisfied and happy, ask yourself this: how strongly do you believe that you can really achieve your goal? It's worth going back to 'The Power of Belief' (Chapter 6).

APP 18 – Your Negative Anchor

Uses: **Creates feelings of repulsion that can be used to put yourself off certain types of food, alcohol, nicotine, people**

Just as it's possible to conjure up good feelings at the flick of a switch (Apps 10 and 15), it's possible to attach bad or unwanted feelings to a similar switch.

Now in case you're wondering why on earth you would want to conjure up bad feelings, let me assure you it can be very useful and will give you greater control over your life.

How convenient would it be to automatically feel repulsion each time you craved chocolate or a cigarette? Or even perhaps ex-boyfriends or ex-girlfriends? It can be very useful.

This app requires you to close your eyes – you can either read through all the instructions before you begin so you'll understand all the steps, or you can invite a friend or colleague to read through the exercise for you.

You'll be asked to squeeze your thumb and middle finger together – for this app you'll need to use those on your non-dominant hand, i.e. the hand that you don't write with.

1. Take a few moments to find somewhere comfortable to sit and make yourself relaxed.

2. Remind yourself of a time in the past when you felt really repulsed by a certain food or drink. (If you are doing this to put yourself off a particular person, remember a time

in the past when they did something disgusting.) Perhaps it was a time when you ate too much and felt sick and bloated; or a time when you were ill and vomited; or a time when you smoked far too many cigarettes and made yourself ill.

3. Close your eyes and take yourself back to that time. See all that you saw, hear all that you heard and feel the feelings that you felt back then.

4. Become aware of what you're seeing in that picture, and make it a bit bigger. Turn the colours up brighter, bolder, stronger, and if there are any sounds in this memory of yours, turn the volume up louder.

5. Make that picture bigger and bring it closer to you.

6. If you can see yourself in that picture (i.e. you're disso-ciated), imagine floating up from your chair and sliding down into the 'you' in that picture.

7. Become the '*you*' and relive this moment once more.

8. Remember this time in the past when you truly felt feel-ings of disgust.

9. As you continue to see this picture in your mind, notice where exactly in your body you're experiencing those feelings of disgust.

10. Locate those feelings and make them spin around even faster, allowing them to spread right through your body from the top of your head to the tips of your toes.

11. Keep running through these steps until you feel those feelings of repulsion begin to peak. (At this point, most people feel as if they are going to be sick and can even start heaving.)

12. As the feeling becomes stronger and stronger, just squeeze together the thumb and middle finger on your non-dominant hand. Squeeze them tightly together, capturing all of those revolting, disgusting feelings.

13. And release. Relax and open your eyes as you come back into the room.

14. Whenever you want to feel this feeling of disgust again, all you're going to have to do is squeeze that thumb and middle finger together once more.

When to use your negative anchor:

- Supermarket shopping – tempted by the chocolate biscuits?

- In the pub being offered crisps and peanuts?

- Second helpings of ice-cream, anyone?

- Another glass of wine?

- The sight and smell of cigarettes.

- Your ex calls and you feel compelled to call back and meet up.

Squeeze your thumb and middle finger together as soon as you think about any of these and you'll get an instant hit of disgust – long enough to enable you to choose a better decision.

Running through this exercise several times a day will ensure that your 'negative anchor' becomes more powerful.

You can attach more feelings to it to make it stronger: each time you come across a food or drink that repulses you, squeeze that thumb and middle finger together again and notice how your desire changes when you use your anchoring technique in the future.

APP 19 – Recalibrating Hunger Signals

**Uses: Getting back in touch with those 'full' and 'hungry'
          signals**

You can do this technique with your eyes open, but most
people find it more powerful with their eyes closed.

1. Remember a time in the past when you felt full, absolutely stuffed. For most people, Christmas Day is what
   usually springs to mind. For you it may be another day
   of celebration – a birthday, perhaps. Perhaps you remember opening a packet of biscuits, a box of chocolates or
   a tub of ice-cream and 'accidentally' finishing the whole
   lot?

2. Close your eyes. Take yourself back to that time now. A
   time in the past when you just ate far, far too much and felt
   really ill as a result.

3. Take a few moments to remember where you were, who
   you were with and perhaps even what clothes you were
   wearing. A time in the past when you just ate too much.

4. See what you saw, feel how you felt, smell those same
   smells and taste those same flavours.

5. Become aware of where in your body you felt those nause-
   ating feelings of being stuffed, bloated and overfed. I'm

guessing you probably didn't feel them in your big toe – so indicate now, by pointing with your finger, where in your body you felt those feelings. Become aware of how and where they move around.

6. Make those feelings move around a bit faster and, as you do, you'll notice those feelings of nausea and bloatedness begin to increase. Take a few moments to really associate with this feeling.

7. This is what feeling *full* feels like. Take note.

And stop . . . open your eyes. Take a break – stand up, stretch and shake your body around a bit. When you're ready you can sit back down again and do some more imagining:

1. Close your eyes, relax and take yourself back to a time when you felt really hungry. Now, for some of you, it may take a few moments to come up with an occasion – but let me assure you, we've all had moments like this. I can personally remember a time when I got caught in a traffic jam on the motorway – there'd been an accident and I was stuck in a queue for over three hours. As I sat in the darkness watching the clock register later and later, I could not only feel my stomach rumbling, I could hear it. Take yourself back to a moment like that now – maybe you were invited to dinner at a friend's and were kept waiting and waiting.

2. See what you saw, hear what you heard and feel how you felt once more. Become aware of where you're sitting in this image, who you are with and the time of day.

3. Notice where inside your body this feeling began and in which direction it travelled. Point to it with your finger and follow it as it moves.

4. Take a few moments to really absorb this memory.

5. This is what *hungry* feels like. Take note.

You can run through this exercise several times and soon you'll begin to get to grips with your body's real and imagined hunger signals and will be able to respond in the appropriate way.

APP 20 – Addiction Breaker

Uses: Creating a loathing for something you feel truly addicted to

Use this technique to specifically target one item you feel out of control around, such as chocolate.

I learnt this technique from Paul McKenna and it's one we used with large audiences at his Weight Loss Seminars. Watching 500 people simultaneously heaving and feeling sick was a sight to behold!

Before you begin this technique, download your Negative Anchor – App 18. It's best to close your eyes to make this technique even more powerful, so read through all the instructions first or get someone to guide you through it by reading it to you.

1. I'd like you to picture the food that you'd like to stop eating altogether. Become aware of whether you're seeing a slice, a portion or the whole thing.

2. Think about this carefully – what's your favourite? Any particular make or brand? Why do you think you're drawn to this food? What makes it so special? This is your 'plate of passion' – see it there clearly in front of you.

3. OK, now let's get rid of that picture.

4. Think about a food that you really hate – something you'd never dream of eating. Some people choose shellfish such

as mussels, cockles or whelks, others pick liver – the smelly green variety they remember from school days or perhaps the sort that oozes blood. Brussels sprouts might do the trick for you, or perhaps even a food that you remember once giving you food poisoning. Yuk.

5. If you really cannot think of anything that turns you off, think of some things that you'd never dream of eating – human hair, for example, or the gunk that blocks your sink every now and again; dog faeces, anyone?

6. Good, now you've got the idea! This is your 'plate of disgust'. Close your eyes and allow your imagination to do all the work for you now.

7. I'd like you to visualise a great big plate of these disgusting things. Bring that plate right up close to you, making it bigger and more colourful and vivid as you do.

8. Now imagine eating bits from this plate. Imagine picking up pieces and popping them into your mouth. See your fingers doing the work and watch as your hand rises up to your mouth.

9. As you chew these items thoroughly, feel the texture as your teeth bite into them. Smell what you smell as you chew, chew, chew thoroughly.

10. Good – then swallow it. Swallow it down hard.

11. And again. Next mouthful – repeat the process again.

12. And take a third mouthful – chewing thoroughly as you go. Keep staring at that plate in front of you, vividly seeing those colours and smelling those ghastly, awful smells.

13. And as you do, have that plate get closer and closer to you. So close in fact that you can feel it touching you. And as it touches you, I'd like you to imagine it *quickly* passing right the way through your body. Feel the 'whoosh' as it passes through and comes out the other side. People often remark that they can feel a rush of air as this happens.

14. Stop now and relax. The 'plate of disgust' has gone away. You're safe now. Pause for few moments.

15. Now give yourself a treat – picture your first plate now. That 'plate of passion', that delicious, favourite food of yours.

16. Bring it closer to you – pick up a piece of your favourite food and bring it up to your mouth. Take a bite.

17. But be careful! As you start tucking into your favourite food, watch what happens. That digusting food is lurking inside! As you bite into your favourite food, bits and pieces from your 'plate of disgust' come oozing out.

18. Look again at that 'plate of passion' and, as you do, fire off your negative anchor – App 18. Squeeze together the thumb and middle finger on your non-dominant hand, releasing yet more feelings of repulsion. Watch as all the food on your 'plate of passion' becomes more and more contaminated with things from your 'plate of disgust'.

19. Go ahead – pick up another piece from your 'plate of passion'. Bite into it and feel a disgusting mixture ooze out onto your tongue once more. Look at the mixture on that plate now, as all your favourite foods become swamped by things from that 'plate of disgust'.

20. Stop, relax your hand and open your eyes. But beware, if ever again in the future you go to eat something from your 'plate of passion', all the items from that 'plate of disgust' will come flooding back into your mind.

21. Enjoy!

APP 21 – Snack Attack

Uses: **To become realistic about the quantity of snacks and unnecessary foods you consume**
To prepare you for the following DIY Gastric Band App

Note: It's useful to download App 18, Your Negative Anchor, before this one.

1. Get a piece of paper and a pen – we're going to do some mental arithmetic. Take your time with this exercise so that you can be accurate.

2. Make a list of all the snack foods you eat unnecessarily. Also include foods you feel out of control around.

3. When you have written them down, calculate how much of these foods you would eat in a day.

4. And now in a week.

5. Now multiply that by four so you can work out how much you would eat in a month. How many bars or packets or cans of drink do you get through?

6. When you have a clear idea of how much of these foods you'd normally consume, allow yourself to visualise how big a pile each of the items you wrote on your list would create. Close your eyes to do this if it helps you.

7. Let's make them bigger now – multiply each pile by three – make it three times bigger so that you can see how much of this stuff you would consume over three months.

8. Once you have a really good idea of how all of these snacks and unnecessary foods mount up, make yourself comfortable with your feet flat on the floor and close your eyes if you didn't do so before.

9. Now see yourself at an airport – perhaps you'll remember one you were at recently.

10. See yourself in the baggage hall, sitting by an empty conveyor belt – it's empty at the moment and not moving.

11. Allow yourself to feel as if you are floating up out of your body and slip into the 'you' you can see sitting there. Become the 'you' at that conveyor belt, so you can now see everything up close, just as you would if you were really there.

12. Take in this picture for a moment.

13. Next, add some sounds to this image of yours. The conveyor belt is starting to move – hear a loud clunk as it begins to rotate. Watch it moving round – it's empty for the moment.

14. And now, things are starting to appear on that conveyor belt. As they do, you realise that rather than suitcases,

what's coming out of the opening is actually those piles of unhealthy, unnecessary foods that you've been eating. See them all spilling out onto the conveyor belt.

15. See all that food – that unnecessary and unwanted food going round and round.

16. Now place on the conveyor belt any foods or liquids you forgot to put on your list. Trust your subconscious to do what is right for you.

17. Watch closely and see all the excess food and drink that you've been consuming for far too long just going round and round on that conveyor belt.

18. Notice what you notice as you see the piles and mounds of unnecessary food just spinning round, right up close to you.

19. And as you watch all this stuff, you begin to realise that if you were to eat any of this right now, you'd be sick, sick, sick. You can make the right choices now.

20. Squeeze together the thumb and middle finger on your non-dominant hand – your Negative Anchor, App 18 – to increase feelings of disgust.

APP 22 – DIY Gastric Band

Uses: **Powerful visualisation to reduce the quantity of food you feel able to eat comfortably**

Note: Before attempting to download your Gastric Band, it's suggested that you first work through App 21, Snack Attack. The more that you practise this technique, the more powerful it will become.

For this exercise, you will need a golf ball and a brightly coloured elastic band. Place them by your side so you'll be able to pick them up when your eyes are closed. Read through this technique to familiarise yourself with it or get a friend or colleague to slowly read the instructions to you.

1. Find a quiet space where you can sit comfortably, with your feet flat on the floor, and relax. It's worth taking a moment to review the relaxation techniques in 'Get in the Right State' (Chapter 8). Choose two of them.

2. Once you feel relaxed and ready to do some visualisation work, I'd like you to just squeeze your hand into a tight fist.

3. This is about the size of your stomach – have a good look at it. Think about all that food you saw on the conveyor belt as you downloaded App 21. Wonder how it all ever managed to fit in – no wonder at times you felt pretty

unwell. Take a few moments to take this in and close your eyes as you do this.

4. As you sit there with your eyes closed, reach to the side and pick up that golf ball and squeeze it tightly, getting a good feel for its size. This is how small the human stomach becomes after it has had a surgical gastric band fitted. Much smaller, isn't it? Spend a few moments doing this.

5. As you clench that golf ball in your hand, reach to the side and pick up the elastic band. Take the band and wrap it around your hand as many times as it will stretch.

6. Now bring your hand over and rest it on your stomach.

7. Picture your stomach shrinking down to the size of that ball. We know that the mind has a powerful effect on the body – we've all heard of people achieving amazing results through their minds, be it healing themselves from diseases or achieving success on the sports field.

8. Keep seeing your stomach shrinking down, smaller and smaller.

9. Now see a band, as tight as the one wrapped around your hand, being fitted around your stomach.

10. And as you see it, so you will feel it. Allow yourself 10–15 of minutes now to fully adjust to this shrinking

stomach of yours and the tightness you'll feel around it from now on.

11. Open your eyes and come back into the room. You can remove the elastic band from around your hand now and let go of the golf ball.

12. Take the elastic band and slip it over your wrist.

13. As long as you keep wearing this band around your wrist, you'll discover that small amounts of food will easily satisfy you from now on.

14. And should you ever find yourself eating more than is necessary, snap the band hard around your wrist and this tight feeling will act as a reminder of the procedure your stomach has undergone. The sensation will put you back in control once more.

15. Spend as long as you feel is necessary to fully absorb these feelings.

End on a positive note – make a bright, bold picture in your mind of how your new future is going to look as the slimmer, fitter, healthier you begins to enjoy life.

Whilst we have spent a bit of time creating 'bad' pictures, I'm going to suggest that from now on you spend your time focusing on 'good' pictures.

'Nothing tastes as good as skinny feels' is quite a well-known saying that has been recently attributed to Kate Moss. Although she was much criticised for saying it, the logic works. When you can get to the stage where something else in your life is much more important to you than food, you will succeed. Be it some new clothes, a relaxing holiday on the beach, a new hobby, the confidence to change jobs or meet new people. It can be anything, but it's worth investing the time to find something that fits the bill.

Find a nice photo of yourself looking slim and good and put it on the fridge. Avoid looking at bad photos of yourself.

APP 23 – Your Mirror Image

Uses: **Enhancing your self-image**
Preparation for social occasions

Note: Before you download this app, come prepared by downloading Your Confidence Anchor, App 10.

Familiarise yourself with this exercise by reading it through several times before you do it. As it's an 'eyes-closed process', you could ask a friend to help you.

Ideally, do this exercise standing in front of a full-length mirror – you may wish to do this in the privacy of your own home. Many people tell me they don't own a full-length mirror precisely for the reason that they can't bear to see themselves. In that instance, I would recommend you use a friend's or perhaps one at your workplace, but do persist as this exercise will help to give you that much needed boost to your self-confidence.

1. Stand in front of your mirror and take a moment to have a look at yourself – notice your posture and the expression on your face. Notice your feelings. We will be comparing how you feel when you look at yourself right now to how you will be feeling at the end.

2. Now close your eyes and remember a specific time in the past when you were paid a compliment. This could be for doing something well at work or a compliment you were

paid for something you did around the house or for something you had recently bought. You don't necessarily need to believe the compliment (you are entitled to disagree) but do choose a person whose sincerity you trust. They meant it, even if you didn't agree with them.

3. As you run this moment through your mind once more, make that image bigger, bring it closer to you, turn the colours up and, most importantly, turn the volume up so you can really hear this compliment being paid once more. Enjoy this moment.

4. When you feel that feeling really strongly, activate your Positive Anchor by squeezing together the thumb and middle finger on your dominant hand.

5. Open your eyes and look into the mirror. Allow yourself to see what the other person saw when they paid you that compliment.

6. Relax your hand now and close your eyes once more. Now, can you think of someone who truly adores you? It could be a loved one, a child or even your crazy dog! Someone out there finds you really attractive – they find you funny and enjoy being with you.

7. As you have your eyes closed, imagine that person is standing right in front of you now. Quite close to you and looking at you with those adoring eyes. See what you see,

hear what you hear and enjoy receiving the adulation that person is sending you through their eyes. Feel the warmth from the positive energy inside their body.

8. As you feel that feeling intensify, squeeze the thumb and middle finger on your dominant hand together once more.

9. Open your eyes and take another look at yourself in the mirror and enjoy seeing yourself with these good feelings inside your body.

10. Send love, approval and positive energy to that person in the mirror. In the past you've looked at that person through your critical eyes – it's time to be a lot kinder to yourself and start sending yourself the love you deserve.

Feeling good on the inside makes us feel better on the outside.

I'd recommend you spend a couple of minutes each day running through this exercise. As good moments – or even funny moments – occur through the day, capture the good feelings on your Positive Anchor. As this strengthens, you'll discover that looking in the mirror as you activate your anchor will mean you become more comfortable with your image – which, after all, is so much more than a collection of thighs, bum and tummy.

Remember, no one will ever criticise you as much as you criticise yourself. If you want people to start being nicer to you, start being nicer to yourself and notice what happens.

APP 24 – Box Up Your Worries

**Uses: Dealing with persistent feelings of worry
           Insomnia due to worrying thoughts**

Worries are very useful things – our minds regularly send us messages telling us that we need to act upon something. Some worries we can deal with immediately, but other times it's just not possible or even necessary to do so. It's the irritating, niggling thoughts that sometimes just don't want to go away no matter how hard you try to push them out of your mind that can simply wear you down.

Worries are emotional messages that our minds send to us, because they're trying to look out for us – they have our best interests at heart. Acknowledging receipt of these messages is often all you need to do to make them go away, for you'll trick your mind into believing that you've taken action.

1. Find a box – it can be an old shoebox or a small, attractively decorated one. Any sort that feels right for you. This is going to be your 'worry box'.

2. Each time you feel worried, get some paper and write down your worry.

3. Think about what might be making you feel like this and write this down too.

4. Once you have finished, fold the piece of paper up and put it into your box. Put the lid firmly on the box and put it away.

5. By writing down your worry, you will have sent an important message to your unconscious mind – letting it know that you have received the message loud and clear and acted upon it.

6. Each time another worry begins to aggravate you, follow the same process. Write it down, fold up the paper and pop it into the box.

7. You'll find the worries begin to evaporate and will cease to keep nagging you.

8. At the end of the week, open your box and empty out the pieces of paper. Read through the worries and be pleasantly surprised as you discover that most of them took care of themselves, without requiring any action from you whatsoever.

Remember – most of the things that we worry about never happen!

APP 25 – Reversing Feelings of Anxiety

Uses: Can alleviate feelings of anxiety whether real, i.e. during an event, or imagined, i.e. before an event

Anxiety can be felt in our bodies in many different ways: some of us feel our hearts pounding away in our chests, a tightness in our throats, a sick or sinking feeling in our stomachs or pins and needles in our legs.

In order for us to 'feel' a feeling it has to keep moving. Let me explain: if I came over to you and stamped on your foot hard, you'd be in pain. And if I came and did it again, you'd feel pain again.

But interestingly, if I came over to you and placed my foot on top of your foot and just kept it there, after the initial reaction, you'd stop feeling the pain. Your foot would habituate to the weight of my foot and would no longer feel it there.

It's the same if I were to stick a small needle in your arm and quickly remove it. You'd certainly feel pain. But if I were to insert the needle and just hold it there, again you'd habituate to it and no longer feel it in the same way.

So – in order for you to be experiencing a feeling of anxiety, we know that the feeling has to be moving around in some way. It travels in a certain direction.

It's no wonder we use phrases such as 'butterflies in the stomach', as this aptly explains what is going on.

Good feelings travel in one direction and bad feelings in another, but you need to discover which way they work for you.

You can perform these steps standing up:

1. Think of something that worries you or makes you feel anxious.

2. Become aware of the anxious feeling as it begins to build up in your body.

3. Notice where it starts and track its movement through your body. It may be moving round in small circles in your stomach or it could be moving up and down your body, or even through your body from front to back.

4. Point to it with your index finger and follow it in the direction of its movement. Imagine giving this feeling a colour – say, red.

5. Once you have established its route, imagine pulling that feeling out your body – use your hands as if you were actually pulling it out. Now that you have it in your hands, turn it around and flip it over.

6. Insert it back into your body and have it travel in the opposite direction.

7. Point to it with your finger once more and track its movements again as it travels in a different way.

8. Give it a different colour – say, blue.

9. Now speed up its movement – have it spin through your body ten times faster than before

10. And as you do this, notice how good feelings take the place of your anxious ones.

11. Think of something that makes you feel good – chocolate ice-cream, perhaps, or a favourite friend. And simply allow this good feeling to grow.

This NLP Spinning Technique is featured here with the kind permission of Richard Bandler

APP 26 – Fast Phobia Cure

Uses: **Erasing phobic responses**

Note: Downloading this app will require you to relive some bad memories before completely erasing them. Ensure that you read through the steps thoroughly before trying them out. If your experience is particularly traumatic to call to mind, it is recommended that you seek out a qualified NLP practitioner to assist you.

This technique works at erasing phobic responses to memories of bad experiences, such as a fear of flying developed after a flight struck by lightning or fear of dogs after being attacked by one.

If you have a fear of snakes, for example, despite having never been in contact with one, your feelings are those of anxiety rather than a phobia and it would be better for you to download Apps 25 and 27.

1. Bring back to mind a memory that causes you suffering as the result of a bad experience.

2. Remember that you were completely safe before the event and are safe again after the event.

3. Now, imagine yourself sitting in a cinema in the front row seeing yourself on the screen in front of you.

4. The film you will be watching is of your bad experience and it's in black and white. It hasn't started yet but you can see yourself there.

5. Now imagine getting out of your seat and walking to the back of the cinema and up into the projection booth.

6. Once here, you can look down onto the screen in safety and watch that movie.

7. It's going to start *before* your bad experience and end *after* it's over and you are safe. Start running it now.

8. Once it has reached the end, freeze it into a still picture.

9. Come out of the projection booth and walk down to the front of the cinema.

10. Imagine floating up into the picture on the screen and become the 'you' in that image.

11. Change the picture into colour and, this time, allow the events to run backwards as you take part in them.

12. This starts at the end of the episode and rewinds back quickly to the beginning of the episode – before your bad experience ever occurred.

13. Do this quickly, so it takes less than thirty seconds.

14. Repeat it again, running this movie with you inside it from the very end all the way back to the very beginning.

15. Add a little circus-style music to accompany these ridiculous events as you see people walking backwards and hear them talking backwards. Everything running backwards.

16. Repeat this again – from the end all the way back to the beginning.

17. End your movie with you, in a place of safety, looking and feeling calm and happy – before the event ever happened.

18. Allow yourself to float out of that screen and back into the cinema seat once more.

19. Look up at the screen and see yourself there, safe and happy.

20. Get up out of your seat and walk back out of the cinema and into the sunshine outside.

After this procedure, you should be able to call to mind the details of your phobia, without feeling the same experience inside your body. You will not forget the event, but you won't feel the same way about it. Repeat this procedure if you feel you need to work on it some more.

The Fast Phobia Cure is featured here with the kind permission of Richard Bandler

APP 27 – Your Calm Anchor

Uses: **Relaxation**
Insomnia
Waiting-room anxiety
Medical procedures

Repeat this technique each day for ten minutes and notice how different you feel after just one week.

1. Make sure you're sitting somewhere comfortable and are unlikely to be disturbed by interruptions.

2. Close your eyes and allow your body to gently begin relaxing. Become aware of your breathing as it slowly travels up and down through your body, and in and out of your nostrils or mouth.

3. Then *blow* out deeply and slowly three times, allowing all your worries, stresses and the strains of life to leave your body through those out breaths.

4. Remember a moment in the past when you felt completely relaxed and stress-free – at peace and calm. Perhaps you'll see yourself relaxing in a nice warm bath, or maybe you'll recall lying on sunny beach on holiday. Perhaps your stress-free moment will be more active – cycling outdoors with the wind blowing through your hair or even horseriding.

Pick a moment that makes you feel happy, content and relaxed.

5. Lose yourself completely in this moment and enjoy the feelings that it gives you.

6. As you keep running this experience through your mind, make it more vivid by making the colours in this image brighter, bolder and stronger. And then make the sounds louder and the picture bigger.

7. Continue making that picture bigger and bring it closer to you – really enjoy this moment of relaxation and make those feelings stronger.

8. As you continue to allow those calming, relaxing feelings to grow and grow just squeeze your middle finger and thumb on your dominant hand tightly together, capturing all those good feelings there. Hold them closed like that for a few moments.

9. Then open your hand and repeat this process at least three more times, taking the time to really enjoy each experience.

Each time you squeezed your fingers whilst feeling those calm, relaxed feelings you were creating a 'calming anchor' for yourself. If ever in the future you find yourself feeling stressed about a particular situation, event or person, all you're going to have to do is squeeze your fingers together in the same way and these good, calm feelings will automatically flood your nervous system.

APP 28 – A Calm Stomach

Uses: **Irritable Bowel Syndrome**
Crohn's Disease
Anxiety-related stomach problems

Note: Also use all the relaxation techniques that are featured in this book as well as downloading Apps 27 and 29 to use on a regular basis.

Whilst experts are still unsure of precisely what causes IBS and Crohn's Disease, what is known is that the mind and body can and do impact on each other – stressful thoughts in the mind trigger unwanted physical responses in the body.

Allow yourself plenty of time for this activity – take at least ten minutes:

1. Take a minute to get comfortable, relax and breathe out deeply three times. (Visualisation exercises are more powerful if you are relaxed, so this is an important point.)

2. Focus down into your stomach area and imagine it becoming warmer and warmer. As it does, allow this warmth to penetrate the rest of your body.

3. Imagine making yourself very small – so small that you can get inside your stomach and walk around inside it. (You may find it easier to do this with your eyes closed.)

4. Picture the inside of your stomach – perhaps it resembles a cave – and become aware of the moisture dripping off the walls. This is the excess acid that causes you problems.

5. See yourself walking around the inside of your stomach with a big, soft sponge. It's very absorbent and you can use it to gently mop up all the excess acid from the walls and the floor.

6. Keep wiping off all the moisture, until there is none left.

7. You can leave your stomach now – imagine becoming your normal size again, and focus on the nice, clean feeling inside.

APP 29 – Your Secret Hideaway

Uses: **Waiting-room anxiety**
Uncomfortable medical procedures
Relaxation on long journeys
Insomnia

Earlier on in the book, I described the benefits of keeping ourselves 'in the moment'. Relishing every bit of a particular moment or experience as you take in more information through your senses can enhance your experience of it.

Of course, it's not ideal to be fully associated with every single experience in our lives – for example a trip to the dentist or going for a blood test. These are the kinds of situations where having your mind elsewhere will serve you very well.

This is the perfect moment to allow your mind to be distracted with other thoughts. Thinking busy thoughts, for example what you need to buy in the supermarket, whom you need to phone, or concentrating on your favourite piece of music, can often do the trick.

Studies have also shown that eating a piece of chocolate whilst having an injection can make it less painful – as the chocolate lights up that pleasure sensor in your brain, it creates a distraction for the pain sensor.

How handy would it be if you had prepared a 'secret hideaway' for yourself in advance? A special place where you could retreat to whenever you needed to?

You may find it easier to do this with the support of a friend

– ask them to read through the steps, slowly and calmly. Or purchase one of my CDs from my website.

1. Begin by choosing one of the relaxation techniques detailed in 'Get in the Right State' (Chapter 8).

2. Then make yourself comfortable, take a nice deep breath and close your eyes.

3. Allow your mind to drift off to a pleasant, peaceful place. A safe, secure place where no one and nothing can bother you.

4. Your secret hideaway may be a place that's outdoors . . . somewhere you've been to on holiday, for example, a tropical beach with fine golden sand, or it could be a place in the countryside . . . perhaps a garden filled with flowers . . . or perhaps a green hillside with views in all directions.

5. Your secret hideaway is somewhere that makes you feel happy and comfortable.

6. It may be a place that's indoors . . . it may be a room . . . a room you have had . . . a room you do have . . . or a room you would like to have. Decorated and furnished in any way you'd like. Candles, rugs, cushions, pictures . . . everything that makes you feel secure and comfortable.

7. Or perhaps your secret hideaway is in the bath, relaxing in a warm, soft tub surrounded by bubbles, soft music and low lights.

8. Your secret hideaway is a place where you can always feel able to let go.

9. See what you see, hear what you hear and feel how good, calm and relaxed this place makes you feel. Enjoy this moment and make it brighter, more colourful, and turn up the volume.

10. Stay in this moment for as long as you would like to and notice the good, calm, relaxed feelings as they spread throughout your body.

11. When you are ready, open your eyes and come back into the room.

Practising this a few times over will make your 'Secret Hideaway' really come alive in your mind. Allow yourself ten minutes or more to do this. Remember the pictures inside our minds control the feelings inside our bodies. So whenever you find yourself in an anxious or worrying situation, you'll be able to drift off to your special place without even needing to close your eyes to get the benefits of relaxation.

Uses: **Painful conditions such as backache, toothache, headache, arthritis, rheumatism**
Childbirth
Injuries that are in the process of healing
Sporting injuries and broken bones

Note: This pain-relief technique is suitable for use with those conditions you have already had diagnosed and are receiving treatment for. Any new and unexplained pain should be referred to a doctor in the first instance.

We're all familiar with stories of people successfully using visualisation and hypnotic techniques to overcome pain – childbirth is one example and procedures at the dentist is another.

Visualisation techniques can be really effective in dealing with chronic pain and promoting healing after surgery or accidents. Because a stressed, tense body will feel pain more acutely, I'm going to recommend that before downloading this app, you take the time to run through all the relaxation techniques earlier in this book. Then you'll be able to make greater use of the powerful effects of this technique.

Any time that you would like to feel more comfortable, you can do so simply by noticing the number that your pain is associated with and then turning it down.

You can choose to have your eyes closed or open for this technique. If you prefer to have your eyes closed, perhaps ask a friend to slowly read through the steps or record your own voice saying the words.

1. Look up in the corner of your mind and notice what number between one and ten represents the pain you are feeling right now.

2. For the purposes of this exercise, let's say it's the number eight.

3. Then just watch . . . watch as the number begins to slowly fade.

4. See it fading more and more into the distance, as a new number appears – the number seven.

5. See the number seven and just notice it for a moment.

6. Then watch as it slowly begins to curl itself up. And as it curls itself up, see the number six appear.

7. See the number six and just notice it for a moment.

8. Watch how it gets blown away by the wind, off into the darkness.

9. See in the darkness a new number appear – this time the number five.

10. As you lower the numbers, you will lower the pain.

11. Watch now how the number five snaps into pieces and drops out of sight.

12. A new number appears – this time the number four.

13. The number you see is the number you feel. The number you feel is the number you see.

14. Some numbers may be skipped altogether as you find yourself able to let go of that pain quicker than expected.

15. Perhaps that number four may vanish in a puff of smoke, leaving behind it a graceful swan gliding by.

16. A lovely white swan, with the graceful long curve of its neck reminding you very distinctly of a number two.

17. Number two gliding by gently.

18. Remember, the number you see is the number you feel and the number you feel is the number you see.

Troubleshooting

As you reach this final chapter, take a few moments now to look back and see how much your thinking has changed and what you've learnt along the way. You now have:

- An understanding of the way your mind works and how the conscious and subconscious minds can begin to work in partnership rather than against each other.

- A set of success strategies enabling you to identify your targets, then shape and define your goal as you truly go for it!

- A set of apps for your mind that you can download as and when you need to, in order to fix your life in a way that you simply haven't been able to before.

But as we all know, life sometimes doesn't always go according to plan, does it? Should you find yourself stuck without understanding why, use this troubleshooting guide, which lists the most common reasons for failure, to point you in the right direction.

1. Is your target unrealistic? Check the timescale you've set and the size of your goal. Chunk it down into smaller, more manageable steps. Really big changes in life can take many months if not years to achieve. The direction in which you're travelling is much more important than the speed at which you go. Give up too quickly and you'll never get there at all.

2. Are you spending too much time in the wrong company? Other people can hold us back, and if you mix with people who are stuck in a negative mindset, you'll find it harder to move forward. Get better friends and begin to model them.

3. Detox your mind from negativity by listening carefully to the words and language patterns that you're using and checking the pictures that they conjure up. Do this on a regular basis.

4. Did you take your eye off the ball and in the busyness of life forget the next steps you were supposed to being taking? Go back to Chapter 7, 'Goal!', and follow the goal-setting procedure.

5. Are you moving the goalposts too frequently? Have you lost half a stone but feel bad because it's still

nowhere near your target weight? Have you recently been promoted to manager but know that the position of director is what you should be aiming for? It's fine to be ambitious, but remember to tune in and appreciate the smaller successes along the way, otherwise you'll always feel a failure.

6. Is your motivation beginning to wane? Learn to give yourself a pat on the back – don't wait for other people to do this. Each evening, write down three things that you could praise yourself for.

7. Are you starting to doubt that you'll ever be successful? Are you reminded of past failures or has someone recently put your efforts down? Go back to Chapter 6, 'The Power of Belief'.

8. Is fear holding you back? As life begins to move in a new direction it's not uncommon to feel nervous and unconsciously give up making changes because it feels more comfortable to do so. Recognise this for what it really is rather than abandoning your goal completely.

9. Is your health and wellbeing letting you down? Are you failing because you're tired, suffering from a lack of energy or an illness? Make this a priority: take better care of yourself and ensure you've plenty of time for relaxation. Once you're back on form, you'll find it so much easier to move forward.

10. And if you find yourself truly stuck and don't know what to do – then *ask*! Start brainstorming and ask friends, family, colleagues or experts on how they would solve this particular problem. Visit libraries, read books and newspapers or search on the internet. Pretty much every problem that exists has already been experienced by someone else and been successfully solved. Track down your solution.

Case Study: Keeping Success in Mind

Susan came to see me as she wanted to fix her panic attacks. She had recently been involved in a car accident and now panicked each time she drove down the same road. Her panic attacks would take over and she'd have to take a detour to get to work. This was adding twenty minutes to her journey time each morning, which simply added to the stress she was feeling.

After working through many of the NLP techniques and strategies, Susan began to feel better and could see that she was finally getter closer to dealing with those panic attacks.

She came to see me again after a month and I asked her how much better things were. She replied, 'I'm just not in control yet. It doesn't seem to be working.'

I asked her to describe to me exactly what was happening. How were her morning journeys going, for instance?

She told me that during her first week, she'd been absolutely fine. Then in the second week, she'd wobbled on a couple of mornings but had managed to control her feelings. Over the next couple of weeks, she'd had one or two bad mornings when she had felt nervous and had even turned her car around on one occasion. She felt a complete failure and wondered if she'd ever overcome this problem.

I pointed out to her that the number of good days was now certainly outweighing the number of bad ones. Yes, Susan agreed, they were.

And it seemed that the 'bad' ones were nowhere near as bad as they had been previously. So perhaps calling them 'bad' was now inappropriate? Again, Susan had to agree and we settled on the new description of 'tricky'.

All in all, when we analysed her journeys it became clear that she hadn't really had any 'bad' mornings at all – not in the way that she was experiencing previously. Presented to her in this way, Susan started to realise that she had been so busy focusing on her failures that she was forgetting to notice her successes.

And we all know what happens when you place your attention, awareness and focus exactly where you don't want it to be. You'll always get more of what you don't want.

Whilst Susan was really only having a couple of 'tricky' mornings now and again, if she continued to focus on these rather than on the successful ones, she could easily fall into the trap of encouraging herself to experience more panic attacks, even though that was the very last thing she wanted.

As we explored Susan's life a little more, I discovered that there were other areas in her life where she found it difficult to see the positive side of things. She admitted that if ever anyone paid her a compliment about her clothes, for example, she would feel self-conscious and immediately brush it off by saying, 'Oh, this old thing – I picked it up in a sale', even if she hadn't.

This lack of self-confidence meant that Susan had programmed herself, over many years, to belittle her achievements and triumphs, however minor they might already be. Her automatic default setting was to shy away from accepting compliments and feeling proud of herself.

I encouraged her to get a notebook and each evening to reflect on the day and to record her successes – however small. It didn't take long for her to begin to automatically seek out the positive aspects of her life rather than the negative ones. Once we set about changing this aspect of her personality, she began to feel more grounded, and those 'tricky' mornings vanished into the past.

So, a final note from me as you embark on your journey of discovery: remember that whatever it is you're planning to fix in your life – however big or small it may seem – once you have set yourself on the right path, be sure to keep looking in the right direction and success will come your way.

Happy fixing!

Alicia

Also by Alicia Eaton: available from www.aliciaeaton.co.uk

For Adults: For Children:

CDs: Books:
Relax Now   Stop Bedwetting in 7 days
Boost Your Confidence
Weight Off Your Mind   CDs:
D-I-Y Gastric Band   Dry Beds Now
Smoke Free   Stop Bedwetting Now
Garden of Your Life Meditation   A Magic Day Out

For more information about NLP visit:
www.purenlp.com
www.anlp.org

For more information about hypnothcrapy visit:
www.general-hypnotherapy-register.com
www.bsch.org.uk